Loyalty to God

An earnest word with those who are sincerely seeking to be right with God and Man.

By
William Telfer

First Fruits Press
Wilmore, Kentucky
c2016

Loyalty to God: an earnest word with those who are sincerely seeking to be right with God and man.
By William Telfer.

First Fruits Press, ©2016
Previously published by the Pentecostal Publishing Company, ©1922.

ISBN: 9781621716013 (print), 9781621716020 (digital), 9781621716037 (kindle)

Digital version at http://place.asburyseminary.edu/firstfruitsheritagematerial/135/

For all other uses, contact:

First Fruits Press
B.L. Fisher Library
Asbury Theological Seminary
204 N. Lexington Ave.
Wilmore, KY 40390
http://place.asburyseminary.edu/firstfruits

Telfer, William.
Loyalty to God : an earnest word with those who are sincerely seeking to be right with God and man / by William Telfer. -- Second edition. -- Wilmore, Kentucky : First Fruits Press, ©2016.
290 pages, [1] leaf of plates : portrait ; 21 cm.
Reprint. Previously published: Louisville, KY : Pentecostal Publishing Company, ©1922.
ISBN - 13: 9781621716013 (pbk.)
1. Christian life--Methodist authors. I. Title.
BV4501 .T45 2016 248

Cover design by Jon Ramsay

asburyseminary.edu
800.2ASBURY
204 North Lexington Avenue
Wilmore, Kentucky 40390

First Fruits Press
The Academic Open Press of Asbury Theological Seminary
204 N. Lexington Ave., Wilmore, KY 40390
859-858-2236
first.fruits@asburyseminary.edu
asbury.to/firstfruits

Sincerely Yours,
William Telfer.

LOYALTY TO GOD

An Earnest Word with those who are Sincerely Seeking to be Right with God and Man.

BY

WILLIAM TELFER,
A Member of the Indiana Conference,
Bloomington, Ind.

"This above all,—to thine own self be true.
And it must follow, as the night the day,
Thou canst not then be false to any man."

SECOND EDITION.

PENTECOSTAL PUBLISHING COMPANY,
LOUISVILLE, KY.

TO MY WIFE

Who has been true and in sympathy with my humble, and, in some respects, difficult ministry.

CONTENTS

PAGE

INTRODUCTION.

This book is life not literature. Its origin is the heart rather than the head. It grows out of convictions, struggles and prayers to know and live the right life. It represents faith in God and victory through faith. The chapters have appeared in religious and other papers. Many, in this form, have had wide circulation. They are introduced here essentially unchanged.

The writer regards them as a series of tracts on important, practical problems of heart, conscience and life. The chapters are placed in this more permanent form for the same reason that the writer preaches—to reach men. The conviction to preach and to write are one, and he sincerely trusts that both are of the Lord.

May the truths which have deeply touched his own heart, life and ministry inspire others to "follow peace with all men, and holiness, without which no man shall see the Lord."

W. T.

Bloomington, Ind., May 29, 1906.

CHAPTER I.

HIS TEST.

The day clerk of a large railroad hotel handled thousands of dollars for his employers, who had no way of knowing what the receipts upon any day should be.

The clerk must be trusted. If honest all was well. If dishonest his employers suffered, till he was found out, then he might suffer.

Occupying the position two years he had the confidence of his employers, who gave substantial evidence of their favor in increased salary.

The few mistakes in his accounts, or in handling money proved his honesty and painstaking effort and served as a bond of confidence between him and his employers.

The members of the firm had been partners for years. They had grown rich and old together.

One, we shall name Mr. Blank, had two sons. The elder, employed as Superintendent of the concern, represented his father. The younger was idle, spending his time around the hotel and was naturally restless.

The two brothers seemed to think that the younger one might, as well, fill the position of clerk. And they set their hearts on getting it.

They made the clerk's position unpleasant. Related as they were to their father and the business their impertinences could not easily be resented. For was he not son and brother? And would not father and brother gladly associate him with them in business? So he was not restrained.

They fumbled in the money drawer, tumbled upside down receipts and bills in the safe, questioning, "what is this," and "what is that?"

And they found fault. Sometimes they had cause and often they had not. But they were irritating as mosquitoes are irritating.

But the crisis came in what follows:

The clerk had charge of the income of the hotel, including the night receipts from all departments, and was book-keeper. The lunch room, news stand, and hotel proper, were open all night to accommodate passengers arriving on night trains.

The money taken during the night was placed in a drawer, which the clerk received in the morning.

Having entire charge of his department he was somewhat careless about taking the proceeds of the night soon as he came on duty. He sometimes waited late in the morning before taking account of it.

On this particular day the noon hour had nearly arrived when he went to the drawer for the envelope containing the cash received during the night.

To his surprise it was missing. Though he tumbled everything around in the search it was not found. Was the money lost? Had it been stolen, or had the night clerk forgotten to leave it in the drawer?

He awakened the night clerk, who said the money was wrapped in a brown paper and placed in the drawer as usual. But it could not be found.

What must he do? Should he replace the money out of his own pocket? Should he make it up out of money from other departments over which he had entire control, and say nothing? Or should he frankly confess that the money was lost, and ask what to do? These things passed through his mind as possible solutions of the problem

At times of warmth the imagination acts with lightning speed. Among other suggestions that came to the clerk's mind, he suspected the superintendent of taking the money. The suspicion gained ground as he remembered seeing him around the money drawer during the morning.

His motive could not be known. The clerk had always been prompt to act upon suggestions he might offer. He did not suspect him of covetous motives or theft, but thought him capable of playing a practical joke. He knew that he wanted his brother in the clerkship, and divined that he would be willing to work a scheme to get him there.

Noon was a busy hour. Trains from all directions stopped for dinner.

When not occupied the clerk was exercised over the missing money. His suspicion of the superintendent seemed so well founded that he looked upon him with contempt, even disdaining to talk with him about it.

Between the arrival of trains, a lull occurred in business, when the clerk went to the room of the proprietor whom he more particularly represented, to explain the loss of the money, but found him suffering an attack of gout, and not in a good humor. "I don't know, or care anything about it," said he, "make it right with the superintendent."

It might be proper to explain that the partner, whom we name Mr. Frank, had previously taken the clerk into his confidence saying: "Mr. Blank is satisfied with you, but would be willing to have his son take your place. And we have offers from rich men who would be glad to have their sons learn the hotel business. We can get them for much less salary than we pay you: But Mr. Blank has one son in the business and I want you to represent me. We believe you are honest and I want you to understand that you are a fixture."

However, receiving no encouragement at a time when he very much needed it, he was thrown upon his own resources and thought, "It is not worth while to play the fool, I would better have this out with the superintendent, and must see him."

Humbling his proud heart, he studied his approach, believing that if he met the superintendent in a wrong spirit or bunglingly, he might deny any knowledge of the money, and once committing himself, would never acknowledge the truth. He concluded it best policy to frankly state the facts.

Cordially received at his room, the clerk began to say that the night money was lost; that the night clerk said the receipts were twelve dollars. He promised, however, to make good the loss, since he might be to blame in not getting the envelope soon after coming on duty.

He had not gotten well started, when the superintendent, fumbling in his pockets, brought out a bunch of brown paper, and in a confused way said, I found this somewhere down there. I don't know what it is. Maybe this is it," handing the package to the clerk.

"Yes," said he, "this is it, and the joke is on me. I have been careless and deserve the rebuke."

"Oh, I do not mean it that way," said the superintendent. "I did not know what was in the package."

"That is all right," said the clerk, with an air of courteous independence. "I understand perfectly, and will improve"—and bowed himself out.

He had not been long in his office when the superintendent entering began apologetically to talk about the package. But the clerk, whose sense of honor had been deeply touched, insisted that he was able to take a hint and would improve by the experience.

From this time the clerk was treated with consideration. The brothers made no more efforts to find fault. And he remained in his position until, by his own choice, he entered another field—his life's work.

CHAPTER II.

A YEAR OF TRIAL

His eleven years in the ministry had been visited with revivals, and he had added to the church rolls. His salary had been uniformly paid, and the benevolences of the church were carefully looked after. He had gradually improved in the class of his appointments and was considered a rising young preacher.

But he was not satisfied. He had a hunger of soul, a dearth of spirit that was disappointing. With ambitions not Christ-like and motives mixed his very efforts to save souls were tinctured with the desire to win success and recognition.

Heart sick he humbled himself at the altar of the church, and received assurance of God's regenerating grace which caused him great rejoicing.

HEART SEARCHING.

A work of heart searching followed, in which he made a consecration of his reputation, money, friends and life for all time, at whatever cost, to the Lord. He promised to preach heaven, hell and holiness as he found the truth in the Bible. The consecration was not easily made, nor was it completed in a moment. Weeks were occupied in the heart-searching process. But he came to the point where he trusted the blood of Jesus to cleanse him from all sin.

In this spirit he went to his new field, meaning in a way that would be honored in bank or on exchange to do the will of God. He saw that while it is easy to break step with God, men can walk with him in righteousness and true holiness all the days of their lives.

HIS NEW FIELD.

His appointment in a beautiful town contiguous to a large city, was composed of sprightly people who proposed to keep pace with the city churches. And so they imitated their worldly ways. The social outranked the prayer meeting; the church theatrical was more popular than the Sunday congregation. Ladies worked in the festival who did not testify to God's saving grace. The social and literary was their department of church work. Perhaps they thought that old fashioned Methodists had talents for testimony and prayer that did not belong to this more cultured age.

A SALOON DRUG STORE.

The pastor was not long in his field until he learned that a leading member, who was the proprietor of a drug store, sold liquor as a beverage, and had been suspected of the practice for thirteen years. He had been before the official board of his church at different times.

After his first round of visits the pastor called upon this member, and requested him to be careful in handling the dangerous drug. Laughing, the member said, "Oh yes, they have been talking to you. They always talk to the new minister. You can believe them if you like." The pastor assured him that he desired only his welfare and the prosperity of the church.

Performing his work the unwelcome news of injuries this member was doing constantly came to him. After a few months he again told the member what was common talk about him and his business, and advsied him to give up his class of young men in the Sunday-school; assuring him that, with the evil reports which would not down, he would do more good not to teach. The important member replied that he had often thought of it. Placing his hand on his shoulder, the pastor said in a kind voice, that could not be mistaken, he believed it would be best.

At this point in the conversation the druggist asked who was talking about his business. The pastor replied, "All classes in and out of the church; high and low; rich and poor; friends and enemies, believe that you sell liquor without license, and that you have done so for years."

THE PASTOR INTERVIEWED.

A few days later the pastor, sitting in his study, was waited upon by two official members. They were conservative, respectable men in the community.

After the civilities of the morning, they laid before him the written resignation of the trustee and Sunday-school teacher, and asked for a meeting of the official board to consider the reports against him.

The pastor replied that the board of trustees was the body to act on the resignation as trustee, and the Sunday-school board on his resignation as teacher; that nothing legal could be done by the official board. But he yielded to their demand to call the whole officiary to examine the case.

They also demanded the names of those who had informed him of the liquor selling, saying, "his enemies are trying to break him down, and other denominations, jealous of our prosperity, would be glad to see us in a muddle."

The pastor was not free to divulge the names, as the information was not to be made public. Theirs was rather a wail of sorrow and disgust that a prominent member should play the hypocrite and dupe the church while the eyes of the community were open to the foul play.

But he promised to see the persons, and if they were willing their names should be known. "But we demand the names," they said. "I cannot give them," he said. "But we came to get them, and will have them." "No," he replied, "I come into possession of facts and no one may know the informants. The law will not require a minister or priest to divulge secrets that come to him in his official capacity."

"See," said they, "what you have gotten yourself into." "I am not sorry of my course. I promised God to be true and not whitewash this violator of law, as has been done in other years. Whatever afflictions attend my course, even to the extent of resigning my church, I told the Lord that I would trust him, and if the worst came it is as near heaven from this city as anywhere."

He asked if the committee desired the persons who had complained invited to the meeting. They agreed that it might do. For they had said that the reports were injuring him, and if not stopped, some people would answer before the court.

The pastor was glad that the druggist would go to the bottom of the trouble. This would increase respect for him. He owed it to himself to stand right before the community. The interview lasted nearly two hours.

THE PASTOR AND HIS WIFE IN PRAYER.

The pastor and his wife alone knelt in prayer. They asked God to place the persons who had complained in his power, so that they would consent to be known as being dissatisfied with the church in retaining in the lead one who held the discipline of his church in contempt.

As they prayed, the conviction deepened that those who were anxious for reform should be brought out of their hiding places, and made to stand openly upon their merits. For the case had assumed such shape that the pastor should not bear the brunt of sins indulged by the church long before he became the preacher in charge. He determined that they should be known. And earnestly prayed God to honor their faith.

It is difficult in a small town for the people to stand, even for the right, against a prominent man or a clique in church, or politics. They usually train together. But to the praise of God be it recorded, these persons consented to attend the meeting, and state their grievances in the presence of the accused.

A MEETING TO INVESTIGATE.

Fearing that they might be prevented from being present, he took precaution to secure their written testimony, to the effect that this church member sold intoxicating liquors in quantities less than a quart, between certain years, contrary to law, and in some cases against their express commands, causing their friends to be drunk, or injuring their families.

A leading official member, who was a physician, and "the power behind the throne," was one of the druggist's drinking patrons. He said, "The committee made a mistake in permitting the complainers to attend the meeting." His wife said, "The doctor was so troubled about it that he spent a sleepless night."

The night for the meeting found no absent members. A number of the informers also were present.

When the meeting was called to order the physician demanded to know why persons not members of the board were there.

"They are here by consent of the committee, who waited on me," said the pastor. The physician thought the official board was able to attend to its affairs.

"These persons are not forcing their presence, but are here at the invitation of the committee to give important information touching the good name of one of its members and the welfare of the church."

But by consent they filed out as unnecessary adjuncts, though representing the most spiritual members of the church.

The pastor opened the meeting by reading Paul's charge to Timothy: "Preach the word; be instant in season, out of season; reprove, exhort with all long suffering and doctrine. For the time will come when they will not endure sound doctrine; but after their own lusts shall they heap to themselves teachers having itching ears. And they shall turn away their ears from the truth, and shall be turned unto fables. But watch thou in all things, endure afflictions, do the work of an evangelist, make full proof of thy ministry."—Titus 4:1-8.

He urged the need of a clean church. A low standard of righteousness causes the ungodly to hold the church in contempt and go without rebuke down to hell.

THE DISCIPLINE ON TEMPERANCE.

He also read the discipline which forbids drunkenness, buying, or selling spiritous liquors, or drinking them, unless in case of extreme necessity. Paragraph 30: "The buying, selling or using intoxicating liquors as a beverage, signing petitions in favor of granting license for the sale of intoxicating liquors, becoming bondsmen for persons engaged in such traffic, renting property as a place in or on which to manufacture, or sell intoxicating liquors."

He then took from his pocket the written statements of the persons who were denied the privilege of being present, and read them one by one.

TESTIMONY.

Much of the testimony would not stand in a court, because the best people who witnessed knew only by the confession of friends of the druggist's liquor selling. They may have come home drunk, or their families may have suffered. And while morally certain that the official sold liquor, they had not seen him in the act, and so, in the eyes of the law, they were not competent witnesses.

The worst elements of society testified what they knew, but being the "worst elements," their word would be doubted because they were the lower classes. But they were made worthless by drink.

The pastor urged the church to rid itself of an evil that made it a byword and hissing among the vulgar crowd, and a grief inexpressible to God's people.

The druggist confessed that he made mistakes, but explained that the physicians prescribed whisky for la-grip. When his old customers complained of la-grip, and the disease was prevalent, he did not compel them to get a prescription, but gave them whisky, as he knew the doctors would do. But promising to obey the discipline, which had been carefully read and expounded in the meeting, his offenses were passed over.

It was suggested that as the investigation was known to the public, the pastor would better state to the congregation what had been the official action.

Preceding the Sunday morning sermon, the pastor, alluding to the meeting of the past week, said: "The drug business is difficult to conduct. Our brother acknowledges making mistakes, but promises to obey the discipline."

The liquor selling trustee was present with his elegant family, and immediately arose, saying: "You leave the shadows upon me."

RISE AND EXPLAIN.

"Please explain the situation fully," said the pastor.

The physician said: "I want this congregation to understand that the official board stands by Brother ——."

"That is true," said the pastor, "make that plain."

Another, addressing the pastor, said: "I will not be quite satisfied unless you acknowledge that you made a mistake."

"I cannot do that," said he; "but I followed the letter and spirit of the Discipline, and am not conscious of acting contrary to the Word of God."

What transpired that Sunday morning deepened the impression that the prominent member was selling whisky without license, supported by his friends, who were leaders in church and society.

We are not to suppose that the church and town people were all intentionally wrong, but that "good kind of people" they had come to make the best of a doubtful case, to say the least. With church interests, lodge interests, business interests, and political and society interests, a net work of influences binding them, the brotherhood were inclined to stand or fall together. If one was a sinner in one direction, another might sin in another. And thus one might not boast over another, or judge another.

Thus, by a law of averaging, they came to indulge one another's foibles and shortcomings, and even to "cover a multitude of sins." It was charity, falsely so-called.

WHAT IT IS TO SPOIL A MAN.

The pastor felt impressed to preach on temperance and the prohibition of the liquor traffic. Concluding his discourse he said: "I am told that there are no saloons in town. But the truth applies to drug stores. It is asked, will a Christian sell whisky for drinking purposes? I reply it is not to be presumed. No, it cannot be. With the vows of the church upon him it is not possible. And yet it comes to my ear from all sources that every drug store in town sells intoxicating liquor as a beverage. The wicked charge it against the church. Parents weep. Wives suffer. And the pious cry, oh! Lord, how long?

"If this be true, we have the Babylonish garment and the wedge of gold—and the curse of God upon our camp.

"If the charge were made against a brother of mine, I would plead with him to cleanse his hands. If he insisted that others would sell, that he needed the money, or trade demanded it; if he persisted in violating his vows, disgracing the church, despising law, tempting the young and working ruin, I would then urge him to leave the church and stand before the community in his true colors as a mammon worshipper, bent on going to hell, and taking as many with him as possible. I should follow him with entreaties to forsake his sins and thus escape the hell of the wicked.

"There is no more need of suspicion resting upon a drug store as being a drinking resort than that a grocery or shoe store sells rum. If any drug store in town will stand on true temperance grounds it will be known before twenty-four hours.

"There are drug stores that will not handle the poison except as medicine."

He drew a picture of what it is to spoil a man: "A fiend may fire a house; an architect is required to build one. An artist may paint a picture; one daub will spoil it. Splendid virtues are required to build a fortune; a robber may wreck it in a night.

"But the house may be rebuilt, the picture painted again, the fortune regained. But what is it to spoil a man with his vast powers and endless life? When once he is ruined who may repair the loss or estimate the calamity?"

TAINTED MONEY.

In the spring, a brother minister visiting in the town asked what the pastor thought of the church receiving money from saloon keepers. He said: "We have four or five jolly saloon fellows, who, at the end of the year, chink in and help pay the preacher's salary.' "

Five dollars from each is considerable when the church is not strong.

They discussed the live question. The pastor insisting

that it was doubtful money, and would better not be received.

Parting from his friend, he felt a check of conscience, as though he had not spoken explicitly in condemnation of the church's complicity with the saloon.

A few weeks passed and he wrote his friend: "Liquor money is blood money, the price of widows' groans and orphans' tears. Received by the church it is hush money. The design is to hoodwink preachers and churches. And the money invested generally succeeds. Saloons do not court a fight with the church. They would quietly close the preacher's mouth with a golden or silver clasp."

A DEEPER CONVICTION.

While writing, the conviction came upon him that he was receiving money from the proprietor of a drug store whom he believed guilty as any saloonist. In a sense, he was not as respectable as the saloon keeper, who pays for his license and goes openly into partnership with the government to spoil men "for revenue only."

This phase of the subject had not presented itself to him before. But the conviction of complicity with the rum power was intense. It came as a revelation, and he could not put it from him.

PRAYER FOR LIGHT.

Falling upon his knees, he attempted to pray, but had no spirit of prayer. It seemed a question of simple honesty. If the druggist received "blood money," to take it as quarterage was to be a "silent partner" in the iniquity. If the preacher were to rebuke him for "making money" out of men's weaknesses and vices he could retaliate: "You need not talk; you get part of your living out of it."

A VISION OF THE CHURCH.

While kneeling, the condition of the church passed before his mind. Three drug stores were owned or rented by persons connected with his church. One was the property of a wealthy Methodist woman, one of the largest payers in the church, and in many respects an estimable woman. But the discipline says our property shall not be rented as a place in or on which to manufacture or sell intoxicating liquors. The proprietor's wife of this drug store was a prominent church worker. The third was the property of another trustee. Rumors were fresh of its ruin of one family.

The confectioner, a church officer, had been labored with for keeping open on Sundays, and selling ice cream, candies and tobacco to boys and girls of the Sunday-school. He said, "I close during church and Sunday-school hours, but I am in the business for all there is in it." And he smiled at pastor, committee, church discipline and State law.

The butcher and the baker, both respectable church members, were the willing tools of those who bought and sold on Sunday. They must keep open or lose trade, and some of of their best customers were members of the church.

The state of the church filled him with alarm: "I shall be ruined. My reputation as a safe pastor will be gone. I cannot be pastor of any church according to the popular idea of conducting churches, for nearly all connive at wickedness, and many have openly wicked members. The radical action may split the church. Sin and holiness won't mix." These thoughts passed through his mind while upon his knees before God. But he had no liberty in prayer. Like a bird driven by wind and pelting storm against the eave of the house, he seemed a helpless sufferer.

One thing was true—he had the light. He could reject or walk in it. To the praise of God, he promised to do right as God gave him to see the right. And he arose and finished his letter.

Going about his pastoral work he inwardly rejoiced that he would return the quarterage and benevolence money paid him by the trustee who had been before the church. This assured him of the presence of the Lord.

LORD, CLEANSE ME.

He prayed day and night, "Lord cleanse me from the love of money; the fear of man and the love of praise." No variety marked the prayer. It was intense, breathed with groanings almost unutterable.

Two or three days passed, when God gave him "an answer of peace." He felt that he was cleansed from the love of money, the fear of man and the love of praise. He could now gladly return the ill-gotten gain which had been laid on the altar of the church. How much to ease conscience, do penance, appear respectable, secure trade, or buy heaven, he knew not and might not judge. But there was abundant fruit by which to know the tree.

Conscious of doing radical work, he feared that the father of lies, or one of his children, might concoct a lie upon him. So placing the money in bank, to be checked to each person, he took a witness as he went to business houses and homes delivering the checks.

He returned to drug stores and Sunday desecrators, all members of his church, and most of them officials representing prominent families, $146.50.

CONFLICTING VIEWS.

This action aroused the community. Some said, "This course is right, he is one of the best men." Others, "What a reflection upon our citizens and church!" And others, "If the money was gotten from wicked business, or in an evil way, the money is not corrupt. The church should use it for God's glory." One said, "The preacher is a good young man, but evidently unbalanced." And he was certainly out of "whack", if the conduct of the church for a generation was in plum with sane judgment and righteousness.

It might be truthfully said, the preacher was not sitting as a model, or bringing a railing accusation against his brethren, but was working out his soul's salvation with fear and trembling, for God was working in him to will and to do of his own good pleasure. And he knew not what to ask as he ought, but the Spirit made intercession for him with groanings which could not be uttered.

The conference year coming to a close, the pastor determined to nominate a good man, in place of this member, on the board of trustees. Strange as it may seem, the Quarterly Conference voted down every nomination. The physician impetuously said, "I would not vote for my own brother to take his place." The position was left vacant. But, the next pastor recognized him as a member of the board, on the technicality that no one had been elected to succeed him.

Official members, usually zealous to pay the pastor and send him to conference with glowing reports, lost enthusiasm, and indeed indicated that they did not care whether the salary was paid or not.

SALARY PAID IN FULL.

To their surprise, a call upon the church for quarterage met a hearty response. Two members who had long felt that the church needed cleaning, said to the pastor, "Have no fear, the salary will be paid." And they divided the deficiency between them, giving him a check in full. They are his friends and true friends of the church to-day.

HIS HANDS CLEANSED.

Returning the ill-gotten gain, the minister's conscience was illumined with the light of God. He felt clear as the angel Gabriel of connection with whisky selling and drinking and Sunday traffic. His spirit grieved, but he felt no responsibility for the evils carried on by church members and winked at by the official board, for he had cleansed his hands and purified his heart.

Tongue cannot describe the sense of cleanness, the freedom from condemnation, the peace of conscience, the minister enjoyed. He walked the streets of the town knowing that rum was working ruin by the consent of the church, but he said: "I cannot help it. I am not guilty. I have done what I could."

Misunderstood and practically rejected by his church, he could sing:

"No storm can shake my inmost peace
While at the fountain drinking;
Since Christ is mine and I am his
How can I keep from singing?'"

THE EVIL CEASED.

The principal offender before one year sold no intoxicants. It was understood that liquor could not be gotten in his store even as a medicine. And this is said to be his practice to this day.

Many of his brethren in the ministry criticised the pastor as hasty and rash. They feared what they called radical methods, and said if more conservative he might touch more people and have a wider sphere of usefulness. But the preacher felt that he was not sent of God to be radical or conservative but to do the will of God.

A LOWER GRADE OF APPOINTMENTS.

More humble members of the conference gave him a warm shake of the hand and a hearty "God bless you!" But his action was not popular, and he took a tumble in the class of his appointments. But he has not doubted that even his disappointments have been God's appointments for him. His bread and water have been sure and his responsibility great as he cared to account for at the day of judgment. His course has been attended with afflictions; but he has had peace of conscience and has been able to give glory to God.

While not fearing criticism, he does not take credit for what some have called a brave act. He says, "It was a conviction upon my soul, evidently wrought by the spirit of God, and not the result of logical processes. I had to follow the light or walk in darkness."

CHAPTER III.

UNSCRIPTURAL MARRIAGES.

A sentiment prevails that preachers have an easy life, wear soft slippers, associate with churchly people, read best literature, get good salaries and are removed from the strife of life as men of the world meet it in business and politics. They are criticised for not leading every social and political reform by those who do not know that the care of a church is as exacting as any secular business.

The following experience shows that the minister's position places him in the forefront of moral battles.

The pastor had been appointed to his charge late in September. It was a two weeks' circuit, with four appointments. Preaching had been maintained for years. And they had revivals, too. But the people felt that something must be wrong, as the church was largely without power.

The minister was no sooner well started in his charge than he learned that certain members were living in adultery; a man having a wife beside his present companion, or a wife another husband, the divorce being secured for other than scriptural causes.

NOT UNDER BAN.

These persons were connected with influential families. Not under ban, but recognized in society, their influence was sought to promote church life. A check upon his spirit, which he did not understand, foreboded unwelcome duty. To preach on divorce would strike terror to the heart of the church, and array influential members against him. He said, "Lord, I am willing to do Thy will." But he hoped there would be another way. He counseled with his presiding elder, who said, "I am sorry." But being "sorry" did not solve the problem of cleansing the church.

He would be prudent, without taking counsel of fear, and was determined to be right. Committing the case to God, he sought divine guidance and watched the providential openings. To labor and wait is a difficult task. We may become impatient and do immature work. Six months were filled with faithful labor of an uneventful character.

A GRASS WIDOW.

While conducting a meeting in the country, a friend assisting him was asked by one of his members what he thought of marrying a "grass-widow." "I can tell you what Jesus said," replied the young man and taking the Bible he read Matt. 19:3-9.

When told of the conversation, the thought flashed through the minister's mind; "Now, I'll preach on divorce." It was settled. From that moment he had no doubt of his duty, nor fear to perform it, though it was a severe task. Closing the meeting, he returned home and wrote a sermon on scriptural divorce.

The Sunday for its delivery was a beautiful day. A large congregation greeted the minister. Among the number an official member and his wife, living in loose marital relations, occupied their usual pew, the second in front of the pulpit.

The pastor was graciously aided by the Holy Spirit in

the delivery of the sermon. The congregation listened attentively, and seemed swayed with various emotions. After the benediction, friends flocked around the loosely-wedded pair, with handshaking and words of sympathy. The preacher was not overrun with greetings to cheer him in a difficult task.

A CLEAR CONSCIENCE.

A high-school teacher, while recognizing the evil, assured the pastor that that kind of preaching would "not take in this town." But the preacher was sustained by a clear conscience and the approving smile of God. The check upon his spirit was removed, the burden gone, and he had rest of soul.

Before the decisive act no expedient satisfied his conscience. Prayer did not remove the burden. He must act. Willing obedience was necessary. He must make himself of no reputation, and expose iniquity in high places publicly as it was practiced. Paul advised Timothy: "Them that sin rebuke before all that others may fear."

When he spoke the truth, regardless of results and fearless of men and devils, the burden of soul departed and never returned. The sermon was preached at each appointment, the iniquity being intrenched in each. Published in the county paper, it was widely read and commented upon.

Some weeks after he invited to church a tardy member enjoying the benefit of easy marriage. In full voice, as if glad of the opportunity, he said: "You know why I do not attend church. I take your sermon as a personal insult." The preacher replied, "I did not mean to be personal. Many people in the community are wrongly married. Loose divorce laws affect the family and throw innocent children out of homes onto unwilling relations and into orphanages. The pastor may not stop preaching because the truth exposes sin. One desecrates the Sabbath, another gambles and bets on elections, others drink, swear and steal. If the preacher may not speak against these evils, his mouth will be effectually closed and he be 'a dumb dog,' unworthy of confidence or support."

A short time has passed in which to estimate the full effect of the righteous course. Some things are evident. The truth was spoken upon a vital subject upon which the pulpit is generally silent. "Truth crushed to earth will rise again" is a beautiful sentiment. But someone must lift its crushed form from the earth, or it will never rise. Truth must be embodied to be a living force.

Unscriptural marriages, endorsed by ministers of the Gospel performing the ceremonies and adding their blessing, for money and popularity, were powerful examples favoring the lusts of the flesh. But the spell of their influence was broken, and a Bible standard is set up for the people.

One effect was to "stir up" the Church. That was the Apostle Paul's life-long business. He turned the world upside down. Finding it wrong side up he turned it on its right side. That was his sole crime.

Six months had not passed until public sentiment changed. Not a minister could be found to publicly defend easy divorce and loose marriage. The question was settled, and settled right. It is but just to say that the immediate offenders still offend. They did not attend church, nor pay quarterage, with one exception, during that pastorate. They remain in the church, a menace and clog to Christian progress. But they are marked people—danger signals to the young and temptable.

CHAPTER IV.

MARRYING AN INFIDEL.

There is a difference between honest doubt and avowed unbelief; between a skeptic and an infidel. One seeks truth, the other vindicates error; one welcomes light, the other loves darkness.

If the question were asked, "Ought a Christian to marry an infidel?" I would answer, unhesitatingly, No.

One who is untrue to God is untrue to himself, and can not be true to any man. Family infelicities and the miseries revealed in thousands of divorce suits prove this.

Three-fourths of the young married women who went to Mr. Moody's inquiry-meetings in Glasgow, Scotland, had ungodly husbands. As girls they were happy Christians. During courtship, their lovers accompanied them to church. After marriage they were unwilling to go. Family cares increased the difficulty. The young mothers lost interest in religion. During a general awakening they would go broken-hearted to the inquiry-room .

Children of infidels will be "free-thinkers." Unbelief suits the "natural man." Infidelity tends downward; it is without restraining power. Such alliances entail evil upon unborn generations. "The fathers have eaten sour grapes, and the children's teeth are set on edge." The iniquity of the fathers is visited "upon the children unto the third and fourth generation of them that hate Me."

The infidel home is not a center of Christian influence. Ministers, evangelists, missionaries, Christian workers, and reformers are not welcome guests. Their prayers and counsels are not sought. Men of liberal views will be there. The immoral may be visitors. The Christian may stand for a time against the tide, but his feet will slip, his strength fail. He is cursed with a curse. The disbeliever may be cultured and wealthy. He may boast of his family, but the case is not altered. Leprosy is in the blood. Gifts increase power. These render him more dangerous because unsuspected. The vicious character, who is the ripe fruit of this system of death, is shunned and hated; while the polished gentleman, sailing, perchance, under guise of "evolutionist" or "higher critic," is admired and courted by the young and inexperienced. But he is a leper.

A PRAYERLESS HOME.

The infidel home is prayerless. His children do not hear the parents' voice in pleading supplication. "The blessing" is not asked at the table. The comfort and guidance of the Holy Spirit are despised. "Prayer, you know, is unscientific. Philosophy has taken its place. This is a day of advanced thought. The light of science has swept away cobwebs of superstition. Every man makes his own god, and answers his own prayer." And thus the mighty power of prayer is lost to the family.

THE BIBLE RIDICULED.

The Bible is ridiculed. "You can't believe the story of Genesis. Man didn't come from the garden of Eden, but from the zoological garden. He did not come from God, but from his father, the ape. Jesus was Divine only as all men are Divine. The Bible is inspired as Homer and Shakespeare and all lofty literature is inspired, and in no other way." The reckless pen-knife of criticism would destroy the Book upon which our civilization is built, and the sacred hopes of mankind for happiness and heaven.

INFIDELITY TEARS DOWN.

How a person can be an infidel in this day of meridian light and heaven-born privilege is a serious question. His attitude is a reflection upon both head and heart. Our civilization is Christian. Churches, schools, colleges, asylums, orphanages, and hospitals, are the product of Christian enterprise. Infidelity endows no college, erects no asylum, builds no hospital, founds no orphanage. It tears down, and would destroy every fair flower of hope. If the fruit of Christianity is not seen, there is cause for the blindness. Ignorance may be responsible and dangerous. Pride of understanding would shut God out of His own world. "The world by wisdom knew not God." Egotism may render its self-centered subject unworthy of friendship, as he is incapable of unselfish love. Sin in the heart or life blinds the eye and paralyzes the soul. The root of unbelief is sin. Confirmed unbelief argues established iniquity, eating, like a cancer, the heart's core. Truth is denied to release conscience and cover evil. Unbelief is not involuntary and innocent as many would like to persuade themselves.

A Christian may not hope to convert the affianced infidel after marriage. Unholy wedlock is a truce with sin, in which the Christian is shorn of his strength. He also lost caste and self-respect. He can not do exploits. He is a cripple.

Refused marriage, the agnostic is placed in full

view of the cross of Christ. The supreme question is thus forced upon his unwilling attention. If he fails to bow to the obligation of a holy life, the Christian may congratulate himself upon the discovery and his happy escape.

The engagement may be broken. The Christian must repent and make proper confession and restitution. A bad vow is better broken than kept. (Matt. xiv, 9.) Married, he may not seek divorce. Jesus recognized but one cause for dissolving the marriage relation. He may take comfort in the apostle's words: "If any brother hath a wife that believeth not, and she be pleased to dwell with him let him not put her away. And the woman which hath an husband that believeth not, and if he be pleased to dwell with her, let her not leave him. For the unbelieving husband is sanctified by the wife, and the unbelieving wife is sanctified by the husband." The position is difficult. But "God is able to make him stand." Let him not lose heart.

The Bible "is the only rule and the sufficient rule, both of our faith and practice." Men may philosophize, but the Book speaks with authority. Hear its voice:

"Blessed is the man that walketh not in the counsel of the ungodly, nor standeth in the way of sinners, nor sitteth in the seat of the scornful."

The "blessed" man walks in wiser counsel. He does not seek the society of the impious, keep company with the wicked, or associate with those who deride God. Much less will he link his life in matrimony with the defamer of God.

UNEQUALLY YOKED.

"Abstain from all appearance of evil. Of the path of the wicked, the Word says, "Avoid it, pass not by it, turn from it, and pass away." "Evil communications corrupt good manners." Is marriage with an infidel possible if the Divine admonitions are obeyed?

"Be ye not unequally yoked together with unbelievers; for what fellowship hath righteousness with unrighteousness, and what communion hath light with darkness? And what concord hath Christ with Belial, or what part hath he that believeth with an infidel? And what agreement hath the temple of God with idols? For ye are the temple of the living God, as God hath said, I will dwell in them, and walk in them; and I will be their God, and they shall be my people. Wherefore come out from among them, and be ye separate, saith the Lord, and touch not the unclean thing ["no unclean thing," R. V.], and I will receive you. And be a Father unto you, and ye shall be my sons and daughters, saith the Lord Almighty."

This Scripture forever settles the duty of the Christian. He may not form unholy alliances in business, politics, or society. This includes marriage. "Come out from among them. Touch no unclean thing," is the fiat of Almighty God. Heaven has spoken, let earth keep silence.

CHAPTER V.

SCRIPTURAL DIVORCE.

"Three hundred thousand divorces have been granted in this country in the last twenty years.

The state of Indiana for the year ending June 1, 1896, issued 24,255 marriage licenses, and, for the same period granted 2,852 divorces. One divorce for every eight marriages in Indiana that year. Owen county, Indiana issued 156 marriage licenses and granted 33 divorces that year, one in five.

Three hundred thousand divorces means that many families brought to an unnatural end. Estimating five to a family 1,500,000 have had their natural home relations destroyed in this country in the last twenty years.

Three hundred thousand of these are women, turned loose to meet life under unfavorable circumstances, liable to evil by the next gale.

Three hundred thousand are men, exchanging homes for boarding houses, charged with passion, often unruly, a menace to purity.

Nine hundred thousand are children without the protection of one and often of either of the parents; a charge upon relatives, or thrown upon the charities of the world, inmates of poor houses or orphan asylums. They often repeat the mistakes of their parents and drift into lives of crime and shame.

To remedy these far reaching evils the State proposes the severance of the marriage tie for several considerations: For adultery, impotency, abandonment, cruel, and inhuman treatment, habitual drunkenness, failure of the husband to provide, and conviction of either subsequent to marriage of infamous crime.

As these laws are administered divorce may be obtained for almost any cause, real or imaginary.

Is the Bible silent, or has God spoken on this important subject? What is the Scriptural cause for divorce?

Matt. 19:3-9. "For every cause." v. 3. Divorce for "every cause" is one of the questions of the ages.

"Male and Female" v. 4. "As he made them one for one, and no more, so the marriage of a single man with a single woman is a law of the race."

"They twain shall be one flesh." v. 5. Husband and wife are more closely related than parent and child. They are one, one in will, affection, spirit, life.

"What God hath joined together let not man put asunder." v. 6. Marriage is of divine origin. It is more than a legal contract. No man, or body of men, can change God's law, which is founded in "infinite truth eternal right and undying love." Any other cause for divorce displeases God, is infidelity to his eternal law.

Infidelity would make God and Moses responsible for this sin and its consequences. vs. 7, 8. How subtle are Satan's devices. Moses did not "command" to give a writing of "divorcement," but "suffered" it because of the "hardness" of their hearts. God is still suffering" a world of iniquity.

"From the beginning it was not so." v. 8. "One for one and no more," was the original design.

"And I say unto you." v. 9. That "I" of divine authority reaches from earth to heaven, extends through all time, is the final word, the last court of appeals. "And I say unto you whosoever shall put away his wife, except it be for fornication, and shall marry another committeth adultery and whoso marrieth her which is put away doth commit adultery. v. 9.

These words have never been misunderstood and they have never been revoked.

"And unto the married I command yet not I, but the Lord, let not the wife depart from her husband. But if she depart, let her remain unmarried, or be reconciled to her husband, and let not the husband put away his wife." 1 Cor. 7:10, 11. "This forbids either party marrying again while both remain alive."

The Apostle again speaks: "For the woman which hath a husband is bound by the law to her husband so long as he liveth; but if the husband be dead, she is loosed from the law of her husband. So then if while her husband liveth, she be married to another she shall be called an adulteress; but if her husband be dead, she is free from that law; so that she is no adulteress, though she be married to another man." Rom. 7:2-3.

How long is the wife bound by the law to her husband: "So long as he liveth." The widow, who is "a widow indeed" may marry again. "If while her husband liveth she be married to another, she shall be called an adulteress." Very plain language. The motley multitudes of earth can understand God's law.

The discipline of the Methodist Episcopal Church is true as the needle to the pole to this serene and severe revelation of God's will.

"No divorce except for adultery, shall be regarded by the church as lawful, and no minister shall solemnize marriage in any case where there is a divorced wife or husband living; but this rule shall not be applied to the innocent party to a divorce for the cause of adultery, nor to divorced parties seeking to be reunited in marriage." Disc. 1896.

A preacher marrying divorced persons contrary to the discipline of his church and the word of God is liable to charges before his Annual Conference for maladministration, and is guilty of a grave crime against the individual. the family and the church of God.

The flood gates of iniquity are open. What can be done to arrest the destructive tide?

Let preachers cry aloud and spare not. The public conscience needs educating. "My people do not consider" is true to-day as when the prophet spoke. Who will declare God's unpopular truth if the preacher, from motives of excessive prudence, which may be "dastardly cowardice," does not? Will the legislator? the politician? the platform lecturer? the secular press? The voice of the preacher should be as the voice of God. Tender as the dew drop, he should be true as the needle to the pole and immovable as the everlasting hills.

EASY PREACHING.

It is easy to declare generally accepted, popular truth. The test of loyalty to Jesus is at the point of declaring God's equally important, unpopular truth.

The laws of the land should conform to God's law. Law educates. The public conscience does not rise higher than the laws upon our statute books. If our laws permitted theft, arson, murder, they would be plead in extenuation of these crimes as our unholy license laws are a strong-hold of the iniquitous liquor traffic. Easy divorce laws encourage hasty, unwise marriages.

Children should be trained for marriage as an epoch

in life. Their associations should be guarded. The parent, qualified to answer every proper inquiry of the child, should leave no morbid curiosity to be satisfied clandestinely. The child, according to his years, should be brought face to face with the facts of his being and destiny. Habits of truthfulness, industry, sobriety, self-reliance, and kindness should be the warp and woof of his life. Christian character is above law.

Revivals of righteousness should be promoted from one end of the land to the other. The preaching of sin and holiness; heaven and hell; law and grace; eternity and the loss of the soul; the new birth and righteous living; death and the judgment day, and the infinite love of Christ, unwilling that any should perish, by spirit baptized ministers is one of God's methods of bringing men to repentance, confession and restitution for wrong doing and lives of holiness, clarifying the moral atmosphere and lifting society to higher levels.

CHAPTER VI.

ONE WOMAN'S INFLUENCE.

A wealthy gentleman of the south, a man of considerable parts, while traveling, met a young lady to whom, after a short acquaintance, he begged leave to tell the sentiments of his heart.

He said, "I have been a widower for two and a half years. I have three little, motherless boys. My intention was not to marry, but you look so much like my wife that I know of no one to whom I could entrust the training of my boys more than to you. If you will consent to marry me I promise you my love and every needed comfort."

She replied, "We can take the matter into consideration." They separated. Letters passed. Another visit, and he renewed his proposal of marriage. Among other considerations, she asked, "Are you a Christian?" He replied, "I am, and belong to the Baptist church."

"FINE CIGARS AND WHISKIES."

They were married. Upon their wedding trip they visited Atlanta, where her husband was completing the erection of a large four-story hotel. He showed, with great pride, his handsome property. They looked at it from the outside, then went through its various stories and halls. At last they came to a side room where were large mirrors, and an elegant counter being placed. Upon the front were printed, "Fine cigars and whiskies." Looking at it from all sides, she asked, "What, and whose is this?" "Oh, its a bar," said her husban.d "Does it belong to you?" "Yes," he said. "Did you not tell me that you are a Christian?" "Yes, I belong to the Baptist church." "Do you think a Christian can sell whisky to ruin other people, soul and body?" "But you can't run a hotel without a saloon." Squaring herself before him, she said, "Look at me, Mr. A. Not a bite of food shall ever go down my throat, not a thread of clothes shall ever go on my back, the money for which comes from that bar. I will die first. I have a small income of about eight dollars a month, and I can work and increase it. I can live economically, and there will be some way to get along, but I will die before I will live on the proceeds of a business that destroys so many lives."

FASTING AND PRAYER DID IT.

When the supper hour came he ordered an elegant bill of fare for two. She sat at the same table and ate crackers, and cheese and water. "What! you are not going to eat that?" "Yes," she replied pleasantly, and refused his elegant food. She spent the night in prayer, weeping and fasting.

Morning came and her husband ordered breakfast for two, thinking, no doubt, that the experience of the night would cure her whims. She sat at the table opposite him, cheerful and attentive, eating crackers and cheese with water.

He hoped that by the dinner hour she would be cured of her pious notion, but she preferred her unpretentious fare, firmly refusing his elegant luncheon, but full of courteous attentions and love in her bearing.

So it was at supper. The second night she spent alone with God in fasting and prayer.

At breakfast she again took her seat before him with her simple fare. Her husband, seeing her pale face and eyes red with weeping, no longer able to endure it, said, "Wife, if you will eat with me, and give me your love as before, I will tear down the bar, or burn it down, or get rid of it in some way."

A generation of genuine, self-denying, godly wives would save a host of goody-good-for-nothing professors of religion, greatly redeem the land of the curse of the legalized saloon, and cause the church of Christ to "arise and shine, her light being come, the glory of the Lord being risen upon her."

CHAPTER VII.

TOO GOOD FOR WHISKEY.

"A gentleman living in Ohio, engaged in the milling business, had $8,000 worth of damaged corn out of which he could not make meal. Two men offered him $3,000 for it, which he accepted. They went into his office to write a draft. One of the men casually remarked, 'A part of the corn can be worked into whiskey.' The observation proved unfortunate in the hearing of the miller, who was not a whiskey man, but up to this time did not know the business of the men. 'Gentlemen,' said he, 'You can't buy my corn to make whiskey.' 'Why, what's that to you?' said they. 'Well, I won't sell my grain to make whiskey,' was the reply. And he didn't. He sent word to the farmers around to come to his mill and haul away the damaged corn."

The circumstance suggests a few remarks:

1. The miller had a right to do as he pleased with his corn, if his freedom did not interfere with other men's rights.

2. His kind of prohibition prohibited.

3. His kind of prohibition cost something besides talk. It cost self-sacrifice. A loss of $3,000.

4. His action would be known for miles and for a generation.

CONVICTIONS NOT THEORIES.

5. His position on the liquor traffic would never be doubted. He had convictions, not notions. A man may

change his theories with every move of the weather vane, but convictions anchor him to principles of righteousness.

6. The Methodist Discipline forbids its members to buy, sell, or use intoxicating liquors as a beverage; to sign petitions in favor of granting license for the sale of intoxicating liquors; to become bondmen for persons engaged in such traffic; to rent property in or on which to sell intoxicating liquors. If these just requirements were carried out by professing Christians the saloon business would suffer an awful loss. "It would fall like Lucifer never to hope again."

7. Men vote prohibition at the polls who vote whiskey in business. Right on election day they are wrong the other days of the year.

A SUNDAY-SCHOOL MAN.

The writer knows a drayman who is an officer in the church, a Sunday-school superintendent, and a Third Party Prohibitionist. This prominent churchman and Prohibitionist drays all of the whiskey and wine and beer from the depot to the saloon of his town, and meekly hauls the empty kegs and barrels and cases back to the depot, to be returned to manufacturers and wholesale whiskey dealers, who will refill and return them.

He is as regular as a clock, and can be depended upon by the whiskey men to be their servant. This is his humble contribution to the whiskey business of his town. He is faithful and has a monopoly of the business. Though he never drinks, the saloon men would not ask a more pliable instrument.

He opens his school every Sunday promptly at nine o'clock with prayer. Monday morning till Saturday night he hauls whiskey and beer and wine, to be used as a beverage, through the streets of his town for the saloons. He is presumably getting intoxicants convenient for the boys and young men of his Sunday-school and church to drink.

This week-day work demoralizes his town more than his Sunday devotions Christianize it. He is like a man building a house with one hand and tearing it down with the other. To change the figure slightly, he is a house divided against itself, which Scripture says "cannot stand."

WHAT WE DO COUNTS.

This professor may work for the saloons under protest. He may say, "I never drink. I hate the business. I wish there was not a saloon in the land." But conscientious scruples avail nothing. Sentiment don't count. What we do lives. Work counts. And he does the devil's work. If the whiskey was not hauled from the depot to the rum shops, and the empty kegs, barrels and bottles returned to the depot, the traffic would stop. If his stopping did not stop the business, it would stop his part of it, "What fools we mortals be!"

DON'T BE A SLAVE.

He may shift responsibility saying, "It is not my business." (His employer also is a prominent church member). "I am only an employee. If I do not my employer's work others will, and I have to live." But he lives his own life. He is no slave. This is a free country. Every man is accountable before the law and God and his conscience for his own acts. "But business and religion won't mix." The worse for such business. Religion will mix with right business and politics, but not with the whiskey trade, so long as Christ and the devil are not on friendly terms. But the wicked world and the worldly church unite heart and hand proposing mutual concessions and harmony for the good of the cause.

"Touch no unclean thing" is Scriptural prohibition. Voting prohibition at the polls is right. This ought ye to do, but not to leave righteousness in every day life undone.

CHAPTER VIII.

"THE SALOON DON'T HURT ME."

"I never drink liquor. None of my people drink, and none of our family have died drunkards," and "the saloon don't hurt me," are expressions frequently heard.

A HIGHER GRADE MAN.

A man may not drink, his sons may not be tipplers, nor his daughters marry drunkards; yet surrounded with saloons it is a question whether any one goes unhurt of the traffic. When this land shall have had one hundred years of prohibition a higher grade man will walk the earth than is common with the sentiments of the people tainted with saloon influence.

"The saloon don't hurt me," says the preacher of the gospel, and yet every year thousands of converts at church altars worship at the shrine of Bacchus before a probation of six months has been served.

WEAK KNEED PREACHERS.

The preacher who speaks delicately and in measured tones against this chief offender of the church, choosing his words with discriminating nicety lest he offend polite ears, can not say: "The saloon don't hurt me." The school teacher who does not, for politic reasons, wear a blue ribbon, sign or pass a remonstrance, saying: "My patrons don't all think alike on this subject; if I was not a public man perhaps I would do differently." That man is wounded in his manhood by the saloon though he may not drink.

LIVE YOUR LIFE.

The railroad employe says privately: "Your temperance work is all right and I endorse it, but I cannot afford to show my colors; the corporation of which I am an employe has issued orders forbidding us taking part in public demonstrations upon which the patrons of the road may be divided." When a full grown man in a free land allows himself to be dictated to in the region of his better nature, suppressing convictions of right and duty, he is at once a lower man though he may not drink.

The business man who is afraid to sign a remonstrance to a saloon license, saying: "My hands are tied; I cannot do anything; I'm in business and dependent upon saloon people and their influence," is a slave to the liquor power, though he may be a total abstainer and an enemy at heart to the saloon.

CUT YOUR BIGNESS THROUGH THE WORLD.

The citizen who acknowledges that there is no evil of the nineteenth century to compare with the American saloon, but bows to public opinion, fails to stand by his convictions of right with the minority, is dominated, good meaning man though he may be, by man's worst enemy and the devil's best friend.

The newspaper that gives an inch of space to a report of a Prohibition convention, carefully edited, and columns to an association of liquor dealers, extolling the members as enterprising citizens and benefactors, is in the grip of the saloon.

The newspaper that systematically suppresses prohibition news, speeches, conventions and statistics, misrepresents or minifies their importance, however much we may extol the liberty of the press, is in the attitude of a slave to his master and dare not call his life his own.

CHAPTER IX.

THE PREACHER'S POLITICS.

A few years ago a friend wrote that his pastor talked and prayed for prohibition, till the campaign waxed hot, and then with his influential members fell in line, and shouted for one of the old party candidates. His pastor's position disappointed him, causing him to lose confidence in his sincerity. He wrote desiring to know his duty toward his pastor, who had been untrue and inconsistent. Should he withhold his support?

Following is the drift of the letter:

If your pastor went back on his convictions, and the declarations of his church, think as charitably of him as possible. We do not all emphasize the same truths. One is impressed with one truth, another feels the power of another truth. This forms different churches and political parties and schools of philosophy.

In politics one emphasizes labor and capital, the tariff, a gold or silver standard, or the liquor problem. Men sincerely differ and train in different political parties.

They do not read the same literature. Some believe in temperance who never read Prohibition papers. Their convictions are not clearly marked. And prohibition reformers may not be "well up" on other vital issues. Some regard prohibition as a moral issue, not having given its political bearing careful thought.

If you have scruples about supporting a preacher voting a license ticket, numbers of Christians have like questionings with reference to supporting Prohibition preachers.

The poet truly says:

"It is good to think
The best we can of human kind."

It is good for ourselves, good for others. We all need to be viewed with charitable eye:

"Then gently scan your brother man,
Still gentler, sister woman;
Though they may gang a kennin wrang,
To step aside is human."

Besides, the scriptures say, "Judge not, that ye be not judged. For with what judgment ye judge ye shall be judged; and with what measure ye mete, it shall be measured to you again." "Who art thou that judgest another man's servant? to his own master he standeth or falleth."

You believe that your pastor has acted a double part, has an overweening desire to be popular, is a moral coward, or from some cause is a weak man. Then do not spend all of your benevolence money on such a man. Others are doing harder, more self-sacrificing work. Give them part of your support.

These humble workers represent righteous, unpopular truth, and are not sufficiently paid. Plain preaching prevents them from being popular. Your pastor is paid a large salary. You can afford to help Christian workers who have courage to stand for the truth and represent your convictions of right. Besides, this is a free country and you have a right to spend the Lord's money in a way that you think will most honor Him.

But you owe something to the support of your pastor and church. You wear out the church carpet, occupy a pew, enjoy the furnace heat, the bright lights, the singing, and use the church hymn books. You are edified by the preaching of a gifted man whose ministry stands in general for clean living and holy dying.

Pay your part, as you esteem him in the light of God's truth, valuable to yourself and the community.

As long as you stay in the church pay your part. And I advise you not to leave the church. Stand by the church and make it better. It represents too much of good, and has done too much for yourself, your family and the world, to be neglected. It is the best institution on earth.

From the church spring the great reforms. Where are found higher utterances on temperance and prohibition than the church voices? Great leaders in temperance and other reforms are born and nurtured there. She may move slowly, great bodies do, but have patience with your mother—she nurtures and gives inspiration to every right movement.

Lastly, how would it do to look to yourself and not eye the preacher? Many are judging preachers who do nothing else. Talk right, live right, vote right, as God gives you to see the right, and let others alone. You are not responsible for the preachers, after doing your duty. Learn the art of letting alone, and that some things are not your business. Cultivate your acre, let other people cultivate theirs, and trust God to take care of His universe.

CHAPTER X.

TOBACCO AND HEALTH.

Merchants, manufacturers, railroad corporations and life insurance companies do not act from sentiment when they forbid employes and patrons to use cigarettes and drink intoxicating liquors.

The following extract is from a letter by the vice president of a life insurance company to one of its agents answering the question whether the company would permit him to write a policy for a youth, sixteen years of age.

"We have never been asked to write any boy under eighteen years of age, but if the boy of whom you speak is well developed, and does not smoke cigarettes, and has a good character for morality and temperance, we could write him on a 'twenty-payment life' plan as at twenty-one."

This letter from a business man representing a great enterprise, without one spark of sentiment in it, speaks in thunder tones to the youth of America: Don't use cigarettes or strong drinks, if you would succeed or if you care for your life.

NICOTINE A POISON.

Nicotine, the principle of tobacco, is poison and should only be taken into the system as medicine. One-seventh of a drop of it on the tongue of a cat is known to have killed it. One-fourth of a drop given to a healthy frog caused it to give one last croak and die.

A little child upon its mother's lap was thrown into convulsions and died by a drop of nicotine falling from a pipe onto its lip.

A distinguished physician said: "Of all the cases of cancer in the mouth that have come under my observation almost every case has been ascribed to tobacco."

Another physician who was superintendent of the insane asylum of Northhampton, Mass., said that one-half of the patients of that asylum lost their intellects through the use of tobacco.

BOYS AND CIGARETTES.

Boys should not use cigarettes. He who does will lose standing in school. His memory will fail. He will not be able to apply himself to his studies. His nervous system will be weakened. He will injure his digestion, poison his blood, hurt his eyes and voice, induce smoker's cancer, and the "tobacco heart." Every boy needs all the sense, health and strength possible to succeed in life. He should do nothing to destroy these. His chances for success are greatly lessened who uses cigarettes.

Certain life insurance companies will not accept cigarette users as risks, and some railroads will not employ them. Many business men reject them. They cannot get a United States army position. They are rejected by the United States navy schools. Some high schools will not accept them as students.

The money spent for tobacco would more than support the churches of the land. Christians should not indulge a habit that is useless, unclean and costs more than the support of the gospel at home and abroad.

CHAPTER XI.

CHARACTER ABOVE MONEY.

Following is the substance of a conversation between a pastor and member of his church who was arranging to travel as salesman for a tobacco manufactory:

Pastor—Have you prayed about the proposition?

Member—No (smiling). I don't know that I have.

P.—But we ought to make our business and all of our plans a subject of prayer. I suppose you know that tobacco contains nicotine, which is a deadly poison —that a mouthful of tobacco spit into a snake's mouth has been known to kill the reptile; that if a person unused to tobacco chews a considerable portion of it he will turn pale and become deathly sick; that it is only by becoming accustomed to it that the human system can tolerate the poison. We may become used to any poison until the body seems to demand the stimulus.

M.—I scarcely know about this.

P.—Whiskey and tobacco are associated. Every saloon in the land sells tobacco and cigars. To do your best work you will need to canvass the saloons.

ON THE DEVIL'S GROUND.

M.—Well, I have thought if Christians would go more into these places they might have more influence.

P.—That depends on their mission. The saloon is the devil's ground, and when Christians go onto his territory he captures them as belonging to him. He has tens of thousands of such prisoners. Besides, nearly every whiskey drinker uses tobacco. The tobacco habit encourages a love for strong drink. Of course, not every tobacco user is a whiskey drinker.

You know that it is a useless, expensive, filthy habit, injurious to the nerves, the digestion, the circulation and the general health.

BUSINESS MEN AND TOBACCO.

Christian men, getting the light, come under conviction and throw away pipe and quid before they get peace of conscience.

Tobacco raisers, manufacturers and salesmen ought to get under conviction and quit cultivating, manufacturing and selling the vile weed, injurious alike to soul and body.

The writer knows grocerymen who are too conscientious to sell tobacco.

It may be used in moderation as medicine, and should be sold only by druggists, as is quinine and strychnine.

BUT MONEY IS NOT ALL.

M.—I can make more money selling tobacco than at anything else.

P.—And for that matter more money can be made selling whiskey than by selling dry goods, groceries, boots or hats, but no Christian man will turn saloon-keeper for "revenue only." Money-making is not the whole of life.

The money standard is too low to settle the high question of right and duty.

CHAPTER XII.

TOBACCO AND HOLINESS.

A gentleman on a train, who knew that the writer was a minister, seemed bent on talking against sanctification, and more anxious to talk than to reason.

Sanctification, of all subjects, should not be spoken of unadvisably with one's lips. But he poured out a volume of prejudice like water from a large hose:

"I do not believe in sanctification. No one can live it: We all sin every day in thought, word and deed. It is all right to grow in grace, but the best people miss the mark continually. And I say, if a man professes sanctification watch him."

Only able to get a word in edgewise it was suggested that he may have heard irresponsible persons who were not able to present the truth in due proportion. Professors may have been ignorant, fanatical or dishonest.

Attempts to pour oil on the troubled water did not quiet the storm. He had an insatiable thirst for the blood of holiness professors.

TOBACCO EFFECTED HIS THEOLOGY.

A lull in the conversation, I turned to my companion with the air of one who would be respectfully familiar enquired what his business was. He meekly replied; *"I am a tobacconist."*

He said no more. One word spoke volumes. And I did not enquire further. The silence was great. It could be felt.

I fell to meditating as the train sped on. Perhaps the

poor fellow has heard holiness preachers fight "the tobacco devil." And every time they thrust the spear of truth through him it went with telling effect into his business and heart.

NO STRAPS ON TRUE HOLINESS PREACHERS.

He may, at first have heard the truth with fear and trembling. Then with admiration for courage, which is common to human nature, he may have rejoiced, with fear, that some one dared to preach the truth, whoever it might offend.

Like Herod, under John the Baptist preaching repentance he may have done "many things"—But the one thing needful—give up his sins—he did not. Herod would not give up Herodias, the tobacconist did not give up his god.

Unwilling to yield, the reaction setting in, doubt and fear would change to anger and hate. Entrenched behind self interest he who feared and trembled would despise and become a full fledged holiness fighter.

Holiness fought his business and exposed the hollowness of his religious profession and he in return opposed holiness as the enemy of his peace and prosperity. And there is a certain inward victory in fighting that the passive nature knows not. This is true whatever the cause.

This may have been the evolution of this soul's experience. Whatever the steps by which he entrenched himself behind its fortifications, we know that everywhere tobacco and holiness are antagonistic.

They do not understand each other and are not in sympathy. When one is in the saddle the other trudges on foot. When one shouts victory the other hangs his head. When one feasts the other hungers. This is universal. They are opposed as light and darkness, as holiness and sin. How can two walk together except they be agreed?

CHAPTER XIII.

A MANAGED CONSCIENCE.

"I would not give much for a man forty-five years old, who has been in business any length of time and cannot manage his conscience," was the remark of a man beyond middle life, who had been reared in a Christian home. A member of church since childhood, he is a regular attendant, and a good financial support of the church. For years he has conducted a wholesale and retail ice cream confectionery in a large city.

But he is a systematic Sunday desecrator. This is the fly in the apothecaries' ointment, sending forth a stinking savour. He panders to the tastes of lovers of pleasure more than lovers of God, and keeps his business open on Sunday to please the public and satisfy his own covetous love of gain.

He does this in violation of a plain command of God. No wonder he is able, after years of evil doing out of the blindness and hardness of his impenitent heart, to utter the sentence attributed to him at the opening of this chapter.

But "one sinner destroyeth much good." He employs young men from country homes. They must be conscientious, honest, industrious; the brightest and best. They must have conscience, but too much of the excellent commodity would not be convenient in his business. They may not steal from him, but must be fundamentally wrong with God. How blind!

A minister was preaching on doubtful and wrong conduct, in the light of God's Word, as the standard of faith and duty. One of the employees of this gentleman, hearing the sermon, was so convicted of the sin of Sunday desecration, that he could not stand erect, but leaned against the church wall as the minister urged him to give up Sunday work and trust God for an opportunity to earn an honest living working six days a week.

His companion said: "You struck him hard all over." Poor fellow! he is well instructed, has high ideals, but is convicted of wrong doing. But he compromises with conscience, saying: "I need the money. This is a good position; the best possible at present, but I hope soon to get a place where Sunday work will not be required."

A man manages his conscience at the peril of manhood, honor, his soul. He breaks himself down in the citadel of his being, virtually saying: "God made me a man, in his own image. I will deface that image. I will degrade my manhood."

The gentleman who has taken his conscience in hand, suffers in his character, as every violator of God's law does. Presumed to be honorable, he is a man of policy. When it pleases him, he is punctiliously attentive to details. But a poor fellow falling into his grasp may find, to his sorrow, that "the tender mercies of the wicked are cruel." Untrue to God, he cannot be true to himself or any man.

But he manages his conscience. He has chosen the world. Money is his god. And he has a measure of success. He has money. He has position. He has friends. He has influence that money brings. But at what cost? The loss of a sensitive conscience, the loss of truth, the loss of freedom, the possible loss of his soul. "What is a man advantaged, if he gain the whole world, and lose himself, or be a castaway?"

A man manage his conscience! As well might the slave presume to domineer his master, the pupil instruct his teacher, the child exact obedience of his parent. Conscience should master the man, and he, its willing, loving slave, should heed its voice; enlightened by the Word, as the voice of God, to his soul. Obedience to its every behest, is his only safety, as it is his crowning glory.

CHAPTER XIV.

SUNDAY OBSERVANCE UNDER DIFFICULTY.

When the General Conference of the Methodist Episcopal Church met in Los Angeles in 1904 many besides delegates took occasion to cross the continent and visit the great West.

There was a man in our party who was not a great preacher or an important ecclesiastic but a modest man occupying a humble place in the Methodist ministry.

The sequel of this story will show that he had convictions and stood by them. Strict views of the Sabbath and especially carrying them out marked him in a way not altogether appreciated by his friends, but they will not soon forget him.

We had traveled from the middle west beyond Denver, and headed for a final run into Salt Lake City were scheduled to arrive there before midnight on Saturday. But at Buena Vista, Utah, upon our engineer starting the engine snap went the coupling of the car, of which our division was part. And we were destined to a delay of ten hours in which we might view snow capped Mt. Harvard, Mt. Yale and Mt. Princeton, and walk restlessly around the village, criticising the railroad management for not getting us out of our dilemma sooner.

But the delay meant that excursionists must travel on Sunday to reach the goal of their ambition—the seat of Mormon power. All on board regretted the detention and thought Sunday travel under the circumstances a necessity.

But our preacher was of conscientious mind and had questionings where others were confident.

Upon going to his berth in meditation and prayer he thought "suppose a proper observance of the Sabbath would require you to not travel to-morrow." "Oh, yes," "but the Lord will not require it. We met with an accident and Sunday travel is a necessity." And so he sought to dismiss doubts which like Hamlet's ghost would not down.

Finally he said, "I will open my heart to consider my duty. God is just. Right is right. Duty is not unreasonable. And I will not fear the consequences." He prayed for guidance and said, "I will know my duty."

The result was that he saw clearly that to be true he must "remember the Sabbath day to keep it holy," which meant that he must not desecrate the day by travel. The command was plain, and his duty seemed plain, though not pleasant to the flesh.

Upon awakening in the morning he consulted the conductor as to a station where he might safely spend the Sabbath. And he prepared his fellow passengers for the step he was about to take, as gently as possible.

A religious editor thought that our situation in passing over this great desert was like a vessel sailing upon the ocean—An ocean steamer is not expected to stop in mid-ocean on Sunday.

A Presiding Elder said that he could not worship a God who would be cruel to his children. He worshipped a God of love.

A minister's wife suggested that if he lived in a city he would use electric and steam cars as necessary to church work.

Another said that when he took charge of a Presiding

Elder's district in Ohio he had conscientious scruples about the use of street cars and trains on Sunday, to meet his engagements. But an older minister advised him that since the situation was different from what it was fifty years ago he would better use the conveniences for the church. If they were in the hands of the devil, God's children should employ them for His glory. Thus he settled the question and his conscience was at rest.

It was also urged that Dr. Blank would preach and conduct religious services on the train.

To the suggestions and criticisms the preacher listened with attention, assuring his friends that while he did not feel free to travel on Sunday he did not sit in judgment on those who did. For if there was difference of opinion as to the manner of observing the day there could be none as to the duty, not to judge one another. The Bible is definite on this point: "Who art thou that judgeth another man's servant? To his own master he standeth or falleth. . . . One man esteemeth every day alike. Let every man be fully persuaded in his own mind: "He that regardeth the day, regardeth it unto the Lord; and he that regardeth not the day, to the Lord he doth not regard it."

Afterwards he said, "None of the criticisms moved me, for I had considered every objection in the darkness of the night as the train sped rapidly on its way, with my heart open to God.

I could not consider Sunday travel necessary. I did not even have to be on time at the General Conference. I should have loved to spend those hours with my brother in his Western home, whom I had not seen for fourteen years, but soon hoped to visit. But that was not a necessity."

Our situation was not analogous to ocean travel for the

train could stop with safety and enjoy the conveniences of civilization. Ceasing to travel did not make God tyrannical because "the Sabbath was made for man," for his highest good. The train men needed the rest of the Sabbath and opportunities of worship. So did the passengers. So do all men.

He had lived in large cities and towns during a ministry of twenty-five years and had not used electric or steam cars. He had gone to appointments on Saturday that could have been reached by train on Sunday morning. He had walked long distances or used private conveyances to avoid the very appearance of evil."

Religious services on the train would not hallow the day if Sunday travel desecrated it. Obedience not sacrifice, is what God demands. Bowing at altars and observing religious ceremonies did not change Baalam's covetous heart or please God. He loved the wages of unrighteousness and caused Israel to sin.

The preacher spent the Sabbath in a small railroad town where work of all kinds was carried on as it generally is throughout the West. He visited a Mormon service and on Monday morning went on his way conscious that he had done the best he knew.

We may say that he was too strict, and literal; that he failed to adjust himself to conditions and become all things to all men. But it may be said in his favor that he thought and acted for himself. He had convictions and, without intruding them upon others, stood for them and stood alone. We sing:

"Dare to be a Daniel,
Dare to stand alone.
Dare to have a purpose true,
And dare to make it known."

But it is easier sung than done.

We condemn the Puritans. We say that they were severe and rigid. The pendulum now swings the other way. We have entered upon a liberal observance of the day. We are not Puritans. We are not bigots. We are not narrow. We boast of liberal views and tolerate all opinions and practices. We believe in freedom, demand large liberty and mistake license for liberty.

But church and state are facing the question of a secular Sunday with the evils that forebode a nation that forgets God.

CHAPTER XV.

CHURCH MEMBERS AND SUNDAY EXCURSIONS.

I do not write for non-church members. While many of the reasons apply to them they are directed to those who profess allegiance to Jesus.

The following reasons against secularizing God's Holy Day should weigh tons on the hearts of professing Christians:

1. The Bible commands ;"*Remember* the Sabbath day to keep it holy." He who goes on Sunday excursions *forgets* the Sabbath day to keep it holy.

2. Worldlings are surprised to see "professors" on Sunday excursions, at least till they get used to it. They say, "What, you here? I didn't expect to see you." They are out of place, but excuse themselves.

3. Church members who ride on these excursions compel workingmen to work on the Lord's day. Engineers, firemen, conductors, brakemen, trainmasters, telegraphers and trackmen must be at their posts to serve the Sunday pleasure seekers .

A Christian has no right to involve others in Sunday desecration. Many railway employes have conscientious scruples against Sunday work. The writer has talked with scores of railroad men, and with scarcely an exception, they deprecate Sunday work.

It deprives them of the opportunity of worship, the society of their families, and needed rest.

4. Railway corporations run excursions on Sunday to make money. They catch the working people. It is not

love of the working man but his money which is the motive power. They have no more moral right to run Sunday excursions than a man has to sell dry goods or groceries, plow, blacksmith or quarry on that day.

Thousands of Christians will not patronize these excursions. Their example is on the right side. If they do not stop "the craze" they stop their part of it.

5. Hundreds of churches are practically emptied during the summer season, by church members going on excursions to witness Sunday base-ball or other attractions of large cities.

A few excursionists try to quiet their consciences by attending church in the city, but the crowd go sight seeing. Some become drunk and disorderly. Others take undue license because away from home and out for a day of pleasure.

6. Those who patronize these excursions have a long, wearisome day, usually get home at a late hour, jaded, disappointed and poorly prepared to commence a week's work. Accidents are frequent in such large, and undisciplined crowds.

7. Church members who patronize Sunday excursions lose the rebuking power of sin. If they lift their voice in condemnation of other evils they are met with the rejoinder: "But you violate the Sabbath day, making it a day of pleasure and convenience. Physician heal thyself."

8. It is argued that Sunday excursions are cheap. Then for money shall we sin? Because we save a dollar does that make it right? If we make God's day one of pleasure seeking and convenience, shall we blame infidelity if it says, "every man has his price. Christians are no better than others. We please ourselves; so do they. When a real issue is involved they dodge. They don't obey their

Bible or conscience any more than we. They are not more honest. They needn't talk. We are as good as they.

9. The example is bad. It misleads and confuses the younger generation. Clear ideals are not presented. A Bible standard is not set up. The young and "outsiders" conclude that there is nothing in Christianity but the name, and, with Shakespeare, they say;

> "What's in a name? That which we call a rose,
> By any other name would smell as sweet."

10. "Enter ye in at the straight gate: for wide is the gate, and broad is the way that leadeth to destruction and many there be which go in thereat: Because straight is the gate, and narrow is the way, which leadeth unto life, and few there be that find it."—Matt. 7:13, 14. Strive to enter in at the straight gate: for many, I say unto you will seek (wish, desire) to enter in, and shall not be able." Luke 13:24. Abstain from all appearance of evil."—1 Thess. 5:22.

It means everything to be a Christian; not much to be a "professor." Self denial is necessary to walk the narrow way. God's "peculiar people" are radically different from mere church adherents. They are full of good works. Their principles, maxims and practices differ from those of the world.

Plainly, as in the days of Moses, is the cry heard, "Who is on the Lord's side? Let him come unto me."—Ex. 32:26.

To all this the excuse is made "but good people patronize Sunday excursions." This reminds me of a story: A holy monk complained that the devil had stolen some of the church's best young men. The devil replied, "I found them on my own ground and took them."

CHAPTER XVI.

THE BLESSEDNESS OF GIVING.

It is blessed to receive.

Behold the happy hearts of children at Christmas time. How they whistle and sing and dance for joy which they cannot all suppress.

With what pride the friend points to the book on the center table, the picture on the wall, the bric-a-brac, the lock of hair—gifts of affection.

The heart sings, "I have friends," and points with pleasure to tokens of love. We cherish the gifts of friendship. They give zest and meaning to life, and make it worth living. They are springs in the desert and songs in the night.

While it is blessed to receive, it is "more blessed to give." The joy of Christmas tide is not all in receiving—it is more than half in giving.

We take for granted that the words, "it is more blessed to give," are true, as he who is "the truth" uttered them. But this lesson is not the first or easiest to learn.

One of the deepest lessons it is learned in the school of life's development. Turn the words over first one way, then the other, and see why "it is more blessed to give than receive." Commencing at the lowest round of the ladder we would say that he who gives is in possession of something. This sign of sufficiency and power supposes him to be provided who gives to another.

In this view would you be the heathen receiving missionary offerings or the Christian who bestows them?

Would you be the recipient of charity or the benefactor to the poor? Would you be "the submerged tenth," the burden and menace of civilization, or the Christian citizen who is taxed for the poverty and crime of our generation?

GIVING INDICATES BENEVOLENCE.

One may, in the vulgar sense, bestow alms without a charitable spirit, but he cannot truly seek the good of others without the quality of goodness. But he may receive love and sympathy, and their expressions in material blessings, and be graceless.

The soul becomes Christ-like in giving. We grow in love by loving; kind by acts of kindness; gentle by being gentle; sympathetic by expressing sympathy.

If giving does not indicate self-victory it is a step in the direction of the conquest. It is a stinging blow to selfishness. Every time an act of giving is accomplished, which carries the soul with it, selfishness cries and benevolence sings.

THIS IS NOT THE WAY OF NATURE.

We would receive. "How will this benefit me? What shall I get in return? You would not expect me to sacrifice and receive nothing. I am looking out for number one. Let every fellow care for himself." Every time one gives the lower nature suffers.

It cries out in pain. Selfishness says, "You hurt me;" Narrowness groans, "You stretch me;" Prejudice whines, "I don't see it so—is nothing coming our way?" The malign passions all suffer, but the higher faculties of the soul, benevolence and nobleness and love, grow and thrive. They make music which is attuned to heaven.

It is observable that the dependent poor become "exacting," as they receive without making adequate returns. They may forget to thank the hand that blesses them, and even talk against their benefactors while demanding aid.

INVALIDS ARE TEMPTED AT THIS POINT.

Their helpless condition makes them receivers, so that they may come to expect favors as their right. But grace will safeguard them. They may forget that the return of gratitude and love is the greatest gifts a human being can bestow, and this is in their power. Its presence in the home is a greater blessing than silver and gold.

Receiving without adequate response leaves the soul undeveloped. Muscles, not exercised, diminish in size, are weak and become paralyzed. Powers of mind or soul unused become weak and diseased.

The fish of Mammoth Cave, not needing eyes in their dark cavern, and consequently not using them, have come at last to be eyeless. It is nature's economy. She hates waste. She will not be mocked. Any faculty not used tends to decay, is atrophied.

IF LOVE LIES DORMANT ENVY AND HATE GROW.

It occupies the soul. Envy devours it. Sympathy not exercised dwarfs and the soul hardens and dies. Giving pierces selfishness through the heart, receiving only may shelter it.

Giving is God-like. God is the great giver. He gave his only begotten Son to die for the world. The Holy Spirit is a gift of the Son of God. He gives freely and withholds no good thing from those who love him.

And lastly,

IF SOME EXERCISE THE GRACE OF GIVING, OTHERS MUST RECEIVE.

If there is a grace of giving there is also a grace of receiving. And this must not be forgotten in balancing things. Many find it harder to receive with grace than to bestow favors. The two go hand in hand in an ideal state. If we give earthly goods and do not receive in kind and measure, we never fail of heavenly grace which is bestowed without stint upon the cheerful giver. And this is greater, as spirit is greater than matter.

CHAPTER XVII.

PAYING THE TITHE.

A prayerful study of Christian giving led to the conclusion that one-tenth of our income belonged to the cause of religion and benevolence. "The tithe is the Lord's."

To consent to pay it was not easy. We were in debt. We already gave as liberally as people in our circumstances. Doubts as to whether God's rule for the Jews applied to Christians presented themselves but we had gotten light upon the Bible rule of giving.

To ease a burdened conscience, we were enabled to lay aside doubts, fears and the spirit of covetousness and dedicate, at least, one tenth of our income to God.

Years have passed. Note the results:

We are at peace on an important christian duty.

We have proven God's promises: "It is more blessed to give than to receive." "Give and it shall be given unto you."

Hundreds of dollars more have found their way into God's treasury.

The whole subject of Christian giving has changed its aspect to us.

Under the old plan, when a benevolence was presented, the question was, "Can we afford it?"

Now, we inquire, "Is this a worthy cause? What part of the Lord's money ought to go to this object?"

Then, giving was sometimes a heavy duty. Now, it is a delight.

Then, it was giving. Now, it is paying.

Light has come upon the Scriptures, which represent us as stewards. We are not proprietors, not absolute owners. "The earth is the Lord's and the fullness thereof. We are his people." We hold what we have in trust. We are appointed to do business for God. How conscientiously we ought to do God's work and pay him his part of the profits.

CHAPTER XVIII.

COVETOUSNESS.

We may forsake gross sins and harbor refined selfishness. Dishonesty is shunned as damning, while evil dispositions infect the spirit and control the life. The drunkard is scorned by those whose hearts are black with avarice and worldly lust.

Inordinate desire to possess may exist without yearning for what is another's.

The man who desired Jesus to divide the inheritance, did not covet his brother's portion. He asked for his own. But earthly concerns crowded out better, holier thoughts. He said: "This is my opportunity. This prophet can adjust my business. Oh! my inheritance; my rights!"

And Jesus looking upon him, said: "Take heed and beware of covetousness."

THE RICH FOOL.

The richer farmer, in the parable, was not coveting another's possessions. "He thought within himeslf, saying, what shall I do, because I have no room where to bestow my fruits? And he said: This will I do: I will pull down my barns and build greater: and there will I bestow all my fruits and my goods.

"And I will say to my soul: Soul, thou hast much goods laid up for many years. Take thine ease; eat, drink and be merry.

"But God said unto him thou fool; this night thy soul

shall be required of thee; then whose shall those things be which thou hast provided?

"So he that layeth up treasure for himself and is not rich toward God."

He was a fool because he forgot that he must die. God was not in all his thoughts. His creed, "the chief end of man is to glorify gold and enjoy it forever," did not satisfy. But he was consistent for he lived his creed. He treated himself as though he was a mere animal. And he stands before the generations of men as "the rich fool" of the Bible. His tribe is not all dead.

DANGER SIGNALS.

This truth occupies a prominent place in the Bible. Danger signals thickly stud the path of life:

"Thou shalt not covet."

"The wicked blesseth the covetous whom the Lord abhorreth."

"Take heed and beware of covetousness."

"No covetous man hath any inheritance in the kingdom of God."

"Mortify, therefore, your member . . . . covetousness which is idolatry."

"They that will be rich, fall into many foolish and hurtful lusts, which drown men in destruction and perdition."

"For the love of money is the root of all evil (a root of all kinds of evil. R. V.) which, while some coveted after, they have erred from the faith and pierced themselves through with many sorrows.

The spirit of greed is the father of many crimes that blacken Bible characters.

THE WEDGE OF GOLD.

Lot selfishly preferred his own to his uncle Abraham's interests, chose the fertile valley of the Jordan for his flocks, and "pitched his tent toward Sodom." We know the harm that came to him and his family.

Achan and the wedge of gold are well set in story and song.

Balaam, a prophet of Israel, loved the wages of unrighteousness and caused Israel to sin. His destiny is wrapped in uncertainty.

Geha i's greed caused him to lie and he was cursed with leprosy.

The rich young man, humbling himself before Jesus to learn the way of life, went away sorrowfully, because "he had great possessions."

Judas betrayed his Lord for thirty pieces of silver, then conscience-stricken, hanged himself, saying, "I have shed innocent blood."

Ananias and Sapphira kept back part of the price of their possessions from the apostles, lied about it, and instantly fell dead by the power of the Holy Spirit.

Covetousness is a spirit, not a circumstance, and is found in every condition of life.

The subject of it may pay his debts, and like Herod under the preaching of John the Baptist, be whipped to "do many things."

THE DRY ROT.

A regular church-goer and payer may be afflicted with the dry rot.

Contributing every week to the support of church,

Sunday-school and missions; giving a little, "about like others," nearly every time, to all the causes, he may be dying, inch by inch, of the "money heart."

FEARS THE POOR HOUSE.

Cupidity manifests itself in anxiety for the future. It says: "I'll grow old and may come to want. I know it is my duty to give but I can't afford it." And he shrinks into his shell more a fossil than a living man.

He complains of aggressive Christianity. "It costs too much. There are too many collections. As to missions we have heathen at home." Asked to help the poor, he replies: "There's no end to giving. It's giving, giving. I can't afford it; charity begins at home." And he might add, "it ends there," with me.

He says, "Benevolence is a waste. Preachers are impractical, begging machines, taking from the town what should be left at home among the poor."

His feelings are wounded by the mention of money. He says, with a sigh: "Money is the bane of the church. If it were not for money we could take the world for Christ." The collection basket "poked under his nose" is an "eye sore." He does not believe in taking collections on Sunday in church. He has scruples against collections taken anywhere upon any other day of the week.

Unfortunate that the church needs money? God made no mistake in causing the church to be dependent upon our means for support. If the cause of religion did not need our money, we need to give.

Naturally selfish, our hearts easily close, become hard and narrow. We need to constantly give to keep our hearts open to the love of God and man. "It is more blessed to give than to receive."

GIVING THE LAW OF LIFE.

God says: "It will save my people from selfishness and develop them in nobility and goodness." And so requires as a law of life, "freely ye have received, freely give."

If forbidden to give time, strength, labor, money, sympathy—everything, we would die spiritually. No greater evil could befall the church than to be placed in a position of independence of our thought and care and love.

The covetous often recur to getting gain. Delighting in possessions, he lusts for more. Like the horse leech, he cries, "Give, give," and is not satisfied.

The words familiar in certain rich farming communities:

"They buy more land—
To raise more corn,
To feed more hogs,
To buy more land,
To raise more corn,
To feed more hogs."

and on, an endless chain, speak of the affections set upon things of earth.

The poet phrases the same sentiment:

"Though flocks and fields increase man's store,
Abundance vainly makes him wish for more."

Conversation reveals character. Money schemes, a favored theme, locate the heart's treasures. "Out of the abundance of the heart, the mouth speaketh." The foxe's tail outside of the hole shows the hunter where the fox is.

No time to read the Bible, attend church, or be alone with God; business and pleasure as excuses for violating the law of God, show the disease, eating as a canker into the vitals.

Envying the rich, looking upon fine houses and appointments with longing eye, indicate the lusting heart. Not desiring his neighbor's possessions, but hankering for as good, or better, is a symptom of the heart disease. Smoke curling from the chimney shows that fire is in the furnace. The hands of the clock indicate the condition of the works within.

MONEY AND HONOR.

Life is lowered by viewing it from the money standpoint. Riches often atone for a man's sins, and make respectable his vices. A "moneyed man," honor or no honor, is often regarded as a valuable citizen. A woman marries a debauchee, but if he is rich, no further questions may be asked. She has done well. It is whispered that the family recently moved into the community has money in the bank, stock in railroads, government bonds, farms and town lots. This is a passport into society, and the church bows a gracious welcome. "Poverty is a calamity, if not a disgrace." Character is disregarded. The dollar is almighty. If you can have both character and the dollar have character, but have money at all hazards.

Millions are dying with consumption and know it not. They protest—deny it, while friends look on dreading the consequence.

Souls are dying ignorant of their disorder. Generosity is dying. Noble impulse is dying. *It is* possible that the church may be manned by dead men? Galvanized they act spasmodically like living men. They act when acted upon. But they are dead—dead in trespasses and in sins.

IDOLATRY.

We look with horror upon heathen bowing to gods of wood and stone. How pitiable their condition! But the Holy Spirit says, covetousness is idolatry. The covetous man says to the "almighty dollar": "Thou art my god," and he bows down and worships. God hates and excludes such characters from his kingdom—Psa. 10:8; Eph. 5:5; Col. 3:5.)

Is there no balm in Gilead? Is there no physician there? Why, then, is not the health of the daughter of my people recovered? Thank God there is a remedy:

Mortification is the cure. "Mortify, therefore, your members. . . . covetousness which is idolatry." To mortify is to destroy, to put to death.

We ask of the condition of a sick friend. It is said that mortification has at last set in. We expect death will soon end the struggle.

REBUKE THE EVIL SPIRIT.

When the old, covetous life asserts itself, rebuke, destroy it. This is to mortify covetousness.

Does duty require of you five dollars, ten dollars, or ten thousand dollars for God's cause? And does an unbelieving heart want to give nothing, or at most, twenty-five cents or one dollar? Rebuke the evil spirit. Say to selfishness: "Get thee behind me, Satan." And let old nature suffer mortification. His death will be the beginning of peace, power and purity in the soul.

Simple trust in the Heavenly Father is the cure. Distrust dwarfs the soul; faith enlarges and ennobles the life.

Lose child-like trust and the spirit enters a cave. The present is dark; the future foreboding. Fears, an ugly brood, infest the life.

"Consider the fowls of the air and the lilies of the field, O ye, of little faith."

CHAPTER XIX.

A RICH POOR MAN.

"I have a member," said a pastor, "who pays twelve hundred dollars taxes, and owns city property and farms and has money in bank. One hundred thousand dollars are his assets. And don't you know that I am the only preacher who has gotten him to give five dollars a year for missions?" "How much does he pay on the preacher's salary?" inquired his friend. "Well, about twenty-five dollars."

"Talking in his home, I urged him to give more to the cause of God as he had been blessed, and there were open doors to enter with money." He replied, "But I cannot afford it. I pay twelve hundred dollars taxes, and that is charity. It is used to care for the poor, the aged and the vicious; to build hospitals and jails, and asylums."

"Oh, but," said his pastor, "Your taxes are not a benevolence. You pay taxes for protection, for road improvement, for bridges, railroads and public buildings and the development of the country."

After a moment's silence and evidently confused as to an answer he replied: "Pastor, I sometimes doubt my conversion and whether I am a real Christian."

This was significant as his personal salvation was not under consideration, and he may not have been given to religious testimony. But he doubted his salvation and feared that he was not right with God. Certainly he lacked peace, purity and spiritual power, and was conscious that his religious duties were doled out much as a slave works under the lash of his master.

He doubted his Christianity! Sinners and saints may have looked at his life and doubted it too, unless the lives of thousands of professors have formed wrong standards of Christianity. But he doubted and well he might, unless his conscience was seared, the Holy Spirit grieved and he a reprobate. Can a man be a Christian and covetous at the same time? It is written, God hates the covetous man. Does God hate the spirit and ways of his own children? Can a man love the world and the things of the world and have the love of God in him? Can he see starvation and suffering and ignorance and crime everywhere prevalent and Christ's kingdom in dire need of men and money, and be a Christian while closing eyes and ears and heart and hands against the calls of God and the appeals of human need?

Such a man is in the position of the rich young ruler who pleadingly inquired of Jesus, "What lack I yet?" The self-centered always feel a "lack." It was the witness of his own spirit, the witness of the Holy Spirit and the witness of the word to his real character. His conscience did not play false to him and Jesus, without apology or reserve, went straight to his heart revealing his deepest need. "One thing thou lackest, go thy way, sell whatever thou hast, and give to the poor, and thou shalt have treasure in heaven; and come, take up the cross, and follow me."

MONEY HIS GOD.

He was selfish. He was covetous. His heart was set on his possessions. He loved money. It was his idol. True, he had many excellent traits of character; He observed the Sabbath day, honored his parents, was chaste, gave a tithe of his income. His morals were rigidly correct.

He would be considered a model church member today. But he was an idolator. Money was his God. He loved this present evil world and was living for it.

When Jesus introduced the knife to cut away the diseased part and give rest and peace by restoring health, he flinched, hung his head, turned around and walked away sorrowfully, "for he had great possessions." He wanted peace of conscience but he coveted gold more.

THE DANGER OF THE RICH.

The danger of the rich is selfishness. Saving and hoarding they cultivate covetousness. It steals stealthily upon them as their pile of gold increases. Though envied by the poor, they often carry heavy hearts and burdened consciences. How many wealthy men in church are without assurance and peace and power because their hearts are set on bonds and stocks and houses and lands? They will be rich. They dig and delve and sweat and live and die for gold. But it will not feed the hunger of the soul.

We must choose whom we will serve. "Ye cannot serve God and mammon," is eternal truth.

And Jesus looked round about, and saith unto his disciples, How hardly shall they that have riches enter into the kingdom of God!

And the disciples were astonished at his words. But Jesus answereth again, and saith unto them, Children, how hard is it for them that trust in riches to enter into the kingdom of God!

It is easier for a camel to go through the eye of a needle, than for a rich man to enter into the kingdom of God.

And they were astonished out of measure, saying among themselves, Who then can be saved?

And Jesus looking upon them saith, With men it is impossible, but not with God: for with God all things are possible.—Mark 10:23-27.

CHAPTER XX.

MAKING MONEY FOR GOD.

We are living in a busy, money-making age. Discovery, invention, commerce all unite to lay their treasures at our feet. Our resources abound. Plenty and even luxury respond to the call of multitudes.

Other generations have labored in poverty. They struggled for the necessities of life in forest, field and mine, under adverse conditions. It may be said of us, "other men labored, and ye are entered into their labors."

It is a question how Christians may use material prosperity and the money-making faculty for God and humanity as it was once a problem to endure hardship and privation in a Christian spirit.

All men are not called to preach—in the technical sense. Men may be Christians and not have gifts and grace necessary to the office and work of the ministry. Paul pertinently asks: "if all were preachers where were the hearers?" He might also add, and the supporters of preachers.

The mass of men will fill their days as workers in material enterprises. They will buy and sell, work quarries and mines, till the soil, construct public highways, invent and exchange the commodities of life.

Some one must do the commerce of the world. The millions will gladly throw their powers of body and soul into the development of the material resources. And they will bless the church and humanity in their life's work.

Anything else that they may do in the Master's kingdom will be incidental.

I have often looked with pain upon men who fail as men, but who succeed as business men. Why is this so common? It may be because they lack instruction. But they place money first. Their aim is money. If they succeed they win money. If they fail it is for want of money.

MONEY OR CHARACTER.

Business masters instead of serving them. Their failure is the result of downright selfishness. They will be rich. That is the rock upon which they split. At any cost they will be rich. They would be honest and rich too, if that were possible. But they cannot let sentiment stand in the way of the goal. With a thousand noble aspirations which cry for recognition they are subjects of one master passion, they will be rich.

At the expense of manhood, honor, truth, benevolence, they will be rich. Indeed these virtues, they think, are but tools with which to build fortunes. "What is the use of being honest if you can't make money? We are not preachers or pious, you know."

Hence so often manhood diminishes as riches increase. The biggest thing about some men is their bank account. And men look at the rich man and say, "He is worth fifty thousand, a hundred thousand, a million dollars. Yes sir, every cent of it.''

Now, money must not be decried. The world's work cannot be carried on without it. It is a noble means of exchange. But what a comment? Poor fellow. Is that all he is worth? Does that represent his assets? Is it the prominent thing that should be said of a man, that he is rich? Who can put a price upon character? What is a soul worth? What's the price of nobility? of honor?

With the false estimate that men place upon life, Jesus looked upon the rich farmer and said, "Thou fool." That's what He thinks of men who accumulate fortunes at the cost of their souls. He had turned himself into a machine to make money, to count and stamp it, when suddenly, without provision, he must meet his God.

The rule seems to be that as men increase in riches they decrease in spiritual grace. "The cares of this world and the deceitfulness of riches, choke the word and he becometh unfruitful."

THE RICH HURT BY RICHES.

John Wesley in his early life knew only three rich men who were not hurt in their spiritual life by their riches. When an old man, referring to the same subject, he said, "When I was younger I knew but three men who did not lose spiritual grace as they became rich. Now, I say, *I never knew one.*

What a statement coming from a careful student of human nature. Every man he had known in a long, public life had been hurt by the accumulation of riches!

MONEY A FETISH.

He meant that the rich are particularly tempted to pride, to think more highly of themselves than they ought to think: to feel contempt for the poor and their inferiors; to impatience. Self-will is fed by riches. A covetous love of the world increases under the hoarding process. They are inclined to slothfulness, ease and self indulgence. They are naturally less self-denying and cross bearing. Consumed with care they hunger and thirst less after God and righteousness. This is the serious hurt of the rich.

When Jesus said, "a rich man shall hardly enter into the kingdom of heaven" the apostles cried out in astonishment, "Who then can be saved?" But Jesus exclaimed: "Children how hard is it for them that trust in riches to enter into the kingdom of God!" When their astonishment knew no bounds he replied: "With men it is impossible, but not with God: for with God all things are possible."

How can the man of secular affairs use his possessions and talents in a Christian way? His gifts are a sacred trust not to be ignored or misused. There is increasing light on the business man's responsibility and use of money. Young men are inquiring how they can serve God in the industries of every-day life. The result is an increasing number in all of the churches who are intelligently doing in bank, on exchange, in market place and field as they believe Jesus would have them do.

The following incident shows how one man employed his opportunities and talent for money-making as a sacred trust. He was God's man to make and use money the same as if he had been God's man to preach, be a missionary to the heathen or do other special, Christian work.

His name, if given, would be known by many in the churches as he has blessed countless good causes. I relate the story of his life as he gave it upon a public occasion:

"I am not a college man, and it was the bitter disappointment of my life that I could not be one. I wanted to go to college and become a minister. I went to Phillips academy to fit. My health broke down, and, in spite of my determined hope of being able to go on, at last the truth was forced upon me that I could not.

"To tell my disappointment is impossible. It seemed as if all my hope and purpose in life were defeated. 'I cannot be God's minister,' was the sentence that kept rolling through my mind.

"I WILL MAKE MONEY FOR GOD."

"When that fact at last became certain to me one morning—alone in my room—my distress was so great that I threw myself flat on the floor. The voiceless cry of my soul was: 'O God, I cannot be thy minister!' Then there came to me as I lay, a vision, a new hope, a perception that I could serve God in business with the same devotion as in preaching, and that to make money for God might be my sacred calling. The vision of this service and its nature as a sacred ministry were so clear and joyous that I rose to my feet, and with new hope in my heart exclaimed aloud: 'O God, I can be thy minister! I will go back to Boston. I will make money for God, and that shall be my ministry.'

"From that time I have felt myself as much appointed and ordained to make money for God as if I had been permitted to carry out my own plan and had been ordained to preach the Gospel. I am God's man, and the ministry to which God has called me is to make and administer money for him, and I consider myself responsible to discharge this ministry and to give an account to him."

CHAPTER XXI.

A NOVEL READER'S EXPERIENCE.

A Christian lady whose conversion occurred under the labors of her pastor, related the following experience:

An inveterate novel reader for years, against the wishes of her husband, she would compel her little child to sit in silence for long periods of time that she might devour the chaffy, if not vile, stuff. Her mental intoxication was not ordinary. One hundred novels a year were not too many for her capacious maw.

She was a nominal church member, and her pastor was conducting a revival. Absorbed with a new sensation, she could not attend the meeting at first, but the conversion of her brother aroused her slumbering conscience and touched her heart. She was soon at the meeting and, with her husband, at the altar.

She there promised God, if he would save her, to give up every sinful thing, and do all for his glory.

Novel-reading—a waste of time, money, and talent, vitiating imagination and heart, intoxicating as whiskey to the drunkard—stared her in the face. It was her foe, her darling sin. Selfishness intrenched itself there. She worshiped at its shine, as thousands of professors of religion are doing.

She saw her sin, repented of it, and said: "God helping me, I will never read another story book or paper." God was talking to her, and she was at last willing to listen and obey.

SHE BURNED THE TRASH.

Going home, she took the stack of novels and piled them onto the fire. They filled the grate more than once.

Her husband plead for the latest one, which he had bought as a Christmas present and which had not been read, but in vain. Its beauty turned to ashes.

A sister entering the home at the time of the burning, argued against such radical measures.

"Don't burn them, and don't read them to excess, but read them moderately."

"No," was the reply, "they have been the enemy of my life, destroying my peace; and I promised God to give up everything displeasing to him, and they must go."

Compromise measures were vai

Her little child, observing the strange procedure, and learning its meaning, clapped her hands and shouted: "Oh, goody, goody, goody."

The Bible has taken the place of the novel in that home. It is read, loved, obeyed.

Her idols burned, she is enabled to worship God, and serve him in spirit and in truth. She can be depended upon to do spiritual work anywhere.

Her testimony is, "I am willing to be led by the Spirit," and her word is believed.

A genuine repentance bears the fruits of reformation. It is a repentance not to be repented of.

She burned the books and papers! Novel reader, by the thousands in the church of God, go thou and do likewise.

CHAPTER XXII.

AN INFIDEL HYPOCRITE.

Hypocrites are not all among professing Christians. Some are in the world, and infidel hypocrites abound.

A pronounced unbeliever asked to subscribe for an infidel paper said: "No, sir, I won't have that paper in my home. It may do for me, but I won't have my family read it." He was not consistent with his profession. While presenting a bold front he was shaky in his unfaith. With pleasure we add that he eventually became a devout believer in Jesus.

Another recognized disbeliever taught his children to discredit Christianity. But upon his death-bed he called his family around him and renounced his infidelity confessing that he had never really believed it.

This surprised his children. The son, who told the facts, was greatly "at sea," as his father had taught him, from childhood that there was nothing in Christianity.

He began to attend church and read the Bible to know the truth. Gradually he groped his way to God. The battle was hard fought against his father's erroneous teachings, the inconsistent lives of church members and his own unbelieving heart. But the Lord graciously helps the willing soul. And to-day he is a believer. He is not the stalwart Christian he might be had his father, true to God, brought up his children in the nurture and admonition of the Lord.

Infidelity lacks the element of reality without which quality there is no true character . As a class infidels are shallow seekers after the truth. They are pretenders influenced by prejudice rather than a sincere desire to know God.

We need not walk in the shadows. Life's problem is not a riddle. We may know. But we will not arrive at certainty by jesting and sophistry.

And spiritual truth comes through the heart. At least the head warms at the fires of the heart. Both are needed but the heart comes first. God says, "My son this day give me thy heart;" "the fool hath said in his heart there is no God." And, "out of the heart are the issues of life."

The unbelieving neither see God in nature nor revelation, but the pure in heart see him everywhere. God resists the proud but gives grace to the humble. Confirmed skeptics need to come down from assumed knowledge and conceit. Continued unbelief cannot be excused. It is willful and wicked; for "he that will do his will shall know the doctrine.' ' Obedience is the key to spiritual truth.

CHAPTER XXIII.

CONFESSION AND RESTITUTION.

During a revival meeting a young man and his wife arose for the prayers of the church.

The second night they kneeled together at the altar. She was soon happily converted. Though friends prayed long and pointed to Christ he was not satisfied.

A minister, knowing his life, asked, "Is there any one whom you should see to make matters right?" He replied, "There is."

He had trouble with a neighbor on account of his turkeys, which were trespassers. His neighbor shot one of the turkeys.

A few days after they exchanged contentious words. Deeply angered, he threw a stone and broke his neighbor's arm in two places.

The injured man received medical attention in a Cincinnati hospital, and though poor, is compelled to hire his work done on the farm. Both families regret the occurrence. They are good citizens and have exchanged work and neighborly kindnesses. A sense of wrong doing burdened his conscience and though he sought peace, could not find it. He was urged to seek reconciliation, as he could not be right with God and wrong with man.

He promised to see his neighbor upon returning home. As he drove three and a half miles in the darkness, over hilly roads, he felt that he could not face the man he had lamed. His soul was weak and troubled and dark. When putting his horse away, and closing the stable door he had the full consent of his mind to meet "his friend, the enemy," and acknowledge the wrong.

WORK THAT WILL STAND IN ETERNITY.

The conflict was over. He quickly crossed the field to his neighbor's house. They had retired for the night. He called time and again. When the surprised man appeared, he readily understood the purpose of the visit and was glad to forgive and be reconciled.

FRUITS MEET FOR REPENTANCE.

The next day his pastor called and found his burden gone. He had peace of conscience, and his face shone with the sunshine of God's love. The burdened soul had at last found an altar of peace. A sense of justice convinced him that he ought to make restitution. He told his pastor that he would pay half of the hospital expenses and, if right, the entire bill.

Under bond for assault and battery, he consulted his neighbor and his lawyer. They quickly settled the difficulty without a lawsuit. He willingly agreed to pay hospital expense, damages and costs.

He and his wife joined the church. They take front seats. A happy family, the voice of prayer is heard in their home. They speak with freedom and joy.

It is to be noted that the church and the community who know the particulars of the case, delight to hear him speak. They believe he is honest, and say: "Brother Blank means what he says and enjoys what he professes. He did right. We have confidence in him."

They would not, could not, believe him or have confidence in his profession of religion, had he, for any cause, failed to make confession and restitution.

An intuitive sense in human nature is quick to respond to honest effort to do the just and right thing.

"He that covereth his sins shall not prosper: but whoso confesseth and forsaketh them shall have mercy."

CHAPTER XXIV.

GET RIGHT WITH GOD.

The minister plead for an honest religion. He enlarged upon the text, "He that covereth his sins shall not prosper, but he that confesseth and forsaketh them shall find mercy of the Lord." The burden of his talk was that a man cannot be right with God and wrong with man.

A young married man who was a member of the church enjoyed the services, expressing a desire to have a good meeting.

After the Bible reading on "True and False Repentance" he took a back seat and fell out of step with the meeting. The evangelist wondered at his changed attitude but later the matter was made plain.

A few years previously he had cultivated an unfenced field of corn. Ordinarily it would need no enclosure because of the stock law of Indiana. As a renter it was not his business to fence the field.

Certain neighbors permitted stock to run at large. He drove them from his field, requesting the owners to observe the law. After repeated trespasses he warned the intruders that he would not be responsible for damage to their stock. They laughed, saying, "We drove those other fellows away, and intend to drive you away." Coming to the point, where, it is said, "Patience ceases to be a virtue," two of their hogs were missing. Whoever might be suspected nothing could be proved. But this professor of religion was responsible for the loss.

His slumbering conscience, now aroused, troubled him.

But he contended with God; "They injured my corn, and I warned them of what they might expect." All to no purpose. His sin was against God, not man primarily. (Psa. 51:4.)

One night after a severe struggle he promised God that he would do right at any cost.

His wife, like Job's, was "a miserable comforter." She said, "You are tempted of the Devil." His father said, "You are going a little too far. You owe those outlaws nothing. Only go on and be faithful to the church."

"Father," he said, "I promised to make wrongs right. I don't have the money, but shall borrow it to pay for the stock I killed." His father seeing his determination loaned him the money to pay for one hog. One of the neighbors had moved into a distant neighborhood.

Determined to do right, his heart was freed of doubts and fears. Peace came before he settled the claims. The Lord took the will for the deed. The meeting closed, and absorbed in spring work he neglected to pay his vows. He may have argued that he did not have the money or time to attend to it. Public opinion may have influenced him, or he may have shrunk from meeting his enemy. But the kingdom is first and the king's business requires haste: "When thou vowest a vow unto God, defer not to pay it; for he hath no pleasure in fools; pay that which thou hast vowed."—Ecc. 5:5.

God came again to his conscience in the quiet of the night. His agony was great. He feared that he might die before morning, for wilful carelessness added to the sin of killing innocent stock and doing to his neighbors as he would not have them do to him. He bitterly repented and promised, if spared, to lose no time in settling the last debt. And "he performed the doing of it." His testimony then was, "All is right. God forgives my sins, and sanctifies my soul. Glory."

SENTIMENTAL PIETY.

There is much sentimental religion. It is false and misleading, powerless and dead. A crying demand exists for truth between man and man. God demands it. Our souls demand it. Men would be happy, but to be right is all important. And he who is right is happy.

CHAPTER XXV.

FUTURE PUNISHMENT.

(Thy Word is truth.—John 17:17.)

Described as:

1. *The Bottomless Pit.*

Rev. 9:1-2.—And the fifth angel sounded, and I saw a star fall from heaven unto the earth: and to him was given the key of the bottomless pit.

And he opened the bottomless pit; and there arose a smoke out of the pit, as the smoke of a great furnace; and the sun and the air were darkened by reason of the smoke of the pit.

2. *A Place of Darkness.*

Matt. 8:12.—But the children of the kingdom shall be cast out into outer darkness: there shall be weeping and gnashing of teeth.

Jude 13.—Raging waves of the sea, foaming out their own shame; wandering stars, to whom is reserved the blackness of darkness forever.

3. *Fire—Everlasting Burnings.*

Isa. 33:14.—The sinners of Zion are afraid: fearfulness hath surprised the hypocrites. Who among us shall dwell with the devouring fire? Who among us shall dwell with everlasting burnings?

Mark 9,43:48.—And if thy hand offend thee, cut it off: it is better for thee to enter into life maimed, than having two hands to go into hell, into the fire that never shall be quenched :

Where their worm dieth not, and the fire is not quenched.

And if thy foot offend thee, cut it off: it is better for thee to enter halt into life, than having two feet to be cast into hell, into the fire that never shall be quenched:

Where their worm dieth not, and the fire is not quenched.

And if thine eye offend thee, pluck it out: it is better for thee to enter into the kingdom of God with one eye, than having two eyes to be cast into hell-fire:

Where their worm dieth not, and the fire is not quenched.

4. *Fire and Brimstone.*

Rev. 14:9-11.—And the third angel followed them, saying with a loud voice, If any man worship the beast and his image, and receive his mark in his forehead, or in his hand,

The same shall drink of the wine of the wrath of God, which is poured out without mixture into the cup of his indignation; and he shall be tormented with fire and brimstone in the presence of the holy angels, and in the presence of the Lamb.

And the smoke of their torment ascendeth up forever and ever: and they have no rest day nor night, who worship the beast and his image, and whosoever receiveth the mark of his name.

5. *The Lake of Fire.*

Rev. 20:14, 15.—And death and hell were cast into the lake of fire. This is the second death.

And whosoever was not found written in the book of life was cast into the lake of fire.

6. *"The Second Death."*

Mark 8:36, 37.—For what shall it profit a man, if he shall gain the whole world, and lose his own soul ?

Or what shall a man give in exchange for his soul?

Luke 9:25.—For what is a man advantaged, if he gain the whole world, and lose himself, or be cast away ?

Jas. 5, 19, 20.—Brethren, if any of you do err from the truth, and one convert him;

Let him know, that he which converteth the sinner from the error of his way shall save a soul from death, and shall hide a multitude of sins.

II.—*Who Are Lost?*

Psa. 9:17.—The wicked shall be turned into hell, and all the nations that forget God.

Mark 16:15, 16.—And he said unto them, Go ye into all the world, and preach the gospel to every creature.

He that believeth and is baptized shall be saved; but he that believeth not, shall be damned.

Rev. 21:8.—But the fearful, and unbelieving, and the abominable, and murderers, and whoremongers, and sorcerers, and idolaters, and all liars, shall have their part in the lake which burneth with fire and brimstone: which is the second death.

Rev. 22:15.—For without are dogs, and sorcerers, and whoremongers, and murderers, and idolaters, and whosoever loveth and maketh a lie.

III.—The Suffering of the Doomed.

Matt. 8:12.—But the children of the kingdom shall be cast out into outer darkness: There shall be weeping and wailing and gnashing of teeth.

Matt. 13:50.—And shall cast them into the furnace of fire; There shall be wailing and gnashing of teeth.

Luke 13:28.—There shall be weeping and gnashing of

teeth, when ye shall see Abraham, and Isaac, and Jacob, and all the prophets, in the kingdom of God, and you yourselves thrust out.

Luke 16:19-31.—There was a certain rich man, which was clothed in purple and fine linen, and fared sumptuously every day:

And there was a certain beggar named Lazarus, which was laid at his gate, full of sores.

And desiring to be fed with the crumbs which fell from the rich man's table: moreover the dogs came and licked his sores.

And it came to pass, that the beggar died, and was carried by the angels into Abraham's bosom: the rich man also died, and was buried;

And in hell he lifted up his eyes, being in torments, and seeth Abraham afar off, and Lazarus in his bosom.

And he cried, and said, Father Abraham, have mercy on me, and send Lazarus, that he may dip the tip of his finger in water, and cool my tongue; for I am tormented in this flame.

But Abraham said, Son, remember that thou in thy lifetime receivedst thy good things, and likewise Lazarus evil things: but now he is comforted, and thou art tormented.

And besides all this, between us and you there is a great gulf fixed: so that they which would pass from hence to you cannot; neither can they pass to us, that would come from thence.

Then he said, I pray thee therefore, father, that thou wouldest send him to my father's house:

For I have five brethren; that he may testify unto them, lest they also come into this place of torment.

Abraham saith unto him, They have Moses and the prophets; let them hear them.

And he said, Nay, father Abraham: but if one went unto them from the dead, they will repent.

And he said unto him, If they hear not Moses and the prophets, neither will they be persuaded, though one rose from the dead.

IV. *Their Doom Everlasting.*

2. Thess. 1:9, 10.—Who shall be punished with everlasting destruction from the presence of the Lord, and from the glory of his power;

When he shall come to be glorified in his saints, and to be admired in all them that believe (because our testimony among you was believed) in that day.

Matt. 12:32.—And whosoever speaketh a word against the Son of man, it shall be forgiven him: but whosoever speaketh against the Holy Ghost, it shall not be forgiven him, neither in this world, neither in the world to come.

Luke 3:17.—Whose fan is in his hand, and he will thoroughly purge his floor, and will gather the wheat into his garner; but the chaff he will burn with fire unquenchable.

Matt. 12:32; Mark 9:45, 46; Luke 3:17; Rev. 14:10, 11.

REMARKS.

1. The figures show that hell is a place of intense agony.

2. The righteous have conscious joy and the wicked conscious misery.

3. The condition of the dead is fixed. There is no repentance after death. I would not risk "a second proba-

tion," nor depend upon "the gospel of eternal hope." There is too much at stake. And I advise my friends to take no such risk. The word says, "There is a great gulf fixed."

4. Their punishment is eternal. We depend not only upon the text but the trend of Scripture. If the joys of the righteous are everlasting the agonies of the wicked endure forever. The same word in the original describes both conditions.

5. We know as much on this subject as any one in the world. No one has ever returned from heaven or hell to give any information. All that is known is revealed in the Bible. Its teachings are explicit. And we can read.

6. Sentiment is not a safe guide by which to settle the question of future retribution. We may say that God is too good to allow men to suffer in the next world. But He is not too good to let them suffer in this world. Men suffer here. They may suffer hereafter. The Bible reveals God's plan of the future. And God's word is the last court of appeals. Nineteen hundred years have passed and there is no new evidence. If learning, infidelity and wickedness of past ages could not destroy the word of God, higher destructive criticism of the present will fall like the hammer upon the anvil.

This writer was nearly wrecked on the rock of liberalism in his early ministry, and felt that to be an honest man he must quit the ministry. His position caused him deep distress of mind. But he was enabled to make a complete consecration to God in which he promised to believe His word and preach sin, repentance, faith, regeneration, sanctification, the judgment, heaven and hell as these are revealed, and leave results with God. In believing and preaching the word he finds peace. And God honors the truth in the salvation of sinners and the sanctification of believers. Glory be to his precious name.

7. The terms of salvation are easy. They are repentance toward God and faith in the Lord Jesus Christ. Any who will, can fulfill the conditions. They are applicable to young and old, rich and poor, learned and ignorant. In emergency on the verge of death the sinner may "look and live," believe with all his heart and be saved with an everlasting salvation. So that we may well inquire "how shall we escape if we neglect so great salvation?" If any are finally lost they will have themselves to blame.

Life is our probationary day. Now is the acceptable time. To-morrow may be too late. Delay is dangerous. The red flag of danger is thrown across every sinner's path.

"Hasten, sinner, to be wise!
  Stay not for the morrow's sun;
Wisdom if you still despise,
  Harder is it to be won."

"Hasten, mercy to implore!
  Stay not for the morrow's sun;
Lest thy season should be o'er,
  Ere this evening's stage be run."

"Hasten, sinner, to be blest!
  Stay not for the morrow's sun;
Lest perdition thee arrest
  Ere the morrow is begun."

CHAPTER XXVI.

THE KIND OF REVIVALS NEEDED.

There are revivals and revivals. Spurious revivals weaken the church and injure the cause of true religion. They set up wrong standards and flood the church with worldlings and unbelievers. They do not increase the spirit of benevolence nor attendance upon the means of grace. They do not settle church difficulties, or promote a forgiving, patient, loving spirit. They do not compel the payment of debts or holy living.

There are revivals on the hand-lifting, card-signing, church-joining plan. They stress the number of additions, great congregations and singing by large chorus choirs. Hundreds are received by the church on scant conviction, repentance and confession of faith. Others stress emotional experience more than intelligent faith in Jesus and holiness of heart and life.

Some revivals are spent when the evangelist packs his valise, and others breathe their last before six weeks.

The revival needed exalts Christ and magnifies the work and office of the Holy Spirit. It creates renewed interest in the Bible and prayer. It leads men to confess their sins and make amends for wrong doing. It promotes a forgiving spirit, and transforms hard hearts into tenderness and love. It creates love for the house of prayer and intense fear and hatred of the card table, the dance hall and the theater. It depopulates the saloon and brothel, and makes happy homes. It sweeps away vile and doubtful things, and multiplies happy witnesses to the pardoning, sanctifying and keeping grace of God. It opens the pocket book for God's cause and throws aside as a defunct institution the church festival and other doubtful expedients to support the gospel.

God give us Holy Ghost, sin-killing, life-giving revivals, the result o, prayer, fasting and separation from the world. May He hasten the time when "the earth shall be filled with the knowledge of the glory of God, as the waters cover the sea." (Hab. 2:14.)

CHAPTER XXVII.

HOW TO PROMOTE REVIVALS.

If ministers were on their knees one hour a day for themselves and their people a glorious change would result in the ministry and church. Two hours would be better. But, at last, it is the spirit more than the form of prayer.

More preachers preach an hour than pray in private an hour. Perhaps it is easier to pray five minutes in public than five minutes in private.

Prayer is work: It is hard work; for we are naturally slothful. But it is paying work. It is glorious work.

We have more instruction in theological schools and journals on how to preach than how to pray. Nevertheless, the apostles said, "Lord, teach us to pray." Though preachers, their principal instruction was in the school of prayer.

Study of methods, books on revivals and biographies of men and women used of God in bringing souls to Christ are helpful, but these will not take the place of prayer. Earnest, agonizing, believing, prevailing prayer is the golden key that unlocks the store house of God's grace.

Pray if you would have revivals; if you would see your children converted or the church quickened. Pray if you seek power. Prayer brings the Pentecost. Study, travel, culture, eloquence, learning, important as they are, will not take its place. Pray, Oh! Pray.

Pastors need the revival spirit. Our slogan is "every

pastor his own evangelist." The evangelistic spirit is being lost in the multiplicity of demands upon pastors. It should be cultivated.

"SOME EVANGELISTS."

But let us not stress this to the detriment of the gifts of others in the church. God has called "some evangelists for the perfecting of the saints; for the work of the ministry; for the edifying of the body of Christ." Emphasizing the office of the pastor, we need not minify the gifts of "some evangelists." Every man in his order.

God honors the gifts of "some evangelists." Many have been saved and the church helped to deeper spiritual life through their holy ministry. "Some evangelists" bless the church a thousand fold. The pastor's sphere of usefulness is enlarged by the faithful service of "some evangelists."

Evangelists cost? So do pastors. But they pay. After "some evangelists" more money remains for missions, pastor's salary and all church work than was available before they came.

IDLERS IN THE VINEYARD.

There are laymen out of debt, with money in bank, complaining at the dearth in the church. They think they abide God's time for an outpouring of the Spirit. Their patience is apathy. They are idle, lounging about. If the Master were to come to-day he would ask armies of such professors, "Why stand ye here all the day idle." Their answer, "No man hath hired us;" that is, placed us on committees, made us members of official boards,

Sunday-school teachers or leaders in church, would not avail.

FAITH WHICH WORKS.

We should prepare for revivals as we prepare for crops and expect an outpouring of the Spirit as we do harvests. Law governs sowing and reaping, whether in the material or spiritual world.

We do not fold our hands and expect a harvest, a house built or business prosperity. Our prayers are answered every day by faith which works.

Prayer for "our children, our neighbors and our neighbors' children" would be gloriously answered by paying Spirit-filled men and women to assist pastors, or hold holiness tent meetings in groves where hundreds might hear the word of Life.

Such men and women are pressing their way into open doors. But many doors are locked and the keys held by covetous hands. Stinginess is a foe to aggressive evangelism. A closed pocket book and revivals of righteousness do not go together. They do not truly pray who do not pay.

Oh, for the application of common sense and business principles to our religious and church life! "The children of this world are wiser in their generation than the children of light." "The harvest truly is great, but the laborers are few: pray ye therefore the Lord of the harvest, that he would send forth laborers into his harvest."

CHAPTER XXVIII.

CONSERVING THE RESULTS OF REVIVALS.

Revivals may be promoted and their results conserved by a free use of the religious press. Tracts and other red-hot revival literature should be widely circulated.

The land reeks with the worthless and vicious in literature. We do not wonder that the heart of the people is weak and ready to faint, and that the love of many has waxed cold, when we consider their mental bill of fare.

TO EVERY ONE HIS WORK.

The children formed into classes for catechetical instruction, and the young into Epworth League Chapters or Christian Endeavor Societies, taking the plan of study and work as the situation allows, the ground of the heart will be preoccupied for Christ. Each member should be treated as an applicant for employment, and assigned a place in the field.

The church is suffering from spiritual dyspepsia from either poor food and overwork, or overfeed and underwork. She presents the spectacle of a large army, many of whom are in camp, many more in the hospital and the few fighting the battles of the cross.

If we would save the convert we must save his environment. It has been said if the church were asked fifty years ago what is the mission of the Christ, the answer would be "to save a lost soul." The same question propounded twenty-five years ago would elicit the reply,

"He came to redeem man, soul, body and spirit," while to-day it is recognized that Jesus Christ came to seek and to save that which was lost, the whole man and his environment.

This larger Christ is to fill this larger life. There is to be room for him in the inn. No crowded apartments, no closed doors, are to exclude him. If ruled out of politics, and told to be satisfied with prayers and the devotions of the church, politics becomes corrupt and a corrupter. If crowded out of business as a pious intruder, preventing sharp bargains, business, instead of a noble means of exchange, becomes an ignoble machine of greed and fraud.

If not a guest of every society, it becomes insincere, a nest of strife and impurity.

The convert sings around church altars, "I am washed and made whiter than snow," but dipped and steeped in impure social and civic relations he is likely to become black as ink.

The church has long recognized its mission to the individual. It must still emphasize the value of the unit. The study of sociological questions attracts increasing attention to the relation of the church to the whole, to the mass of society.

Christ discoursed with the individual; he also took a whip of small cords and purified the temple. He dealt with the classes and the masses of the people.

Municipal reforms point to the larger scope of church life.

The redeemed soul needs a redeemed environment.

CHAPTER XXIX.

CONVERSIONS THE YEAR ROUND.

"The average church is without sufficient vitality to give birth to spiritual children the year round." It may have conversions when the forces are rallied, but through weakness soon falls from the supreme effort. But is it possible? Jesus answers, "All things are possible to him that believeth." "The things which are impossible with men are possible with God."

"Emerson states a universal truth, "We get what we live for." Church socials, literaries, concerts, the product of inventive brains and busy hands interest people and supplement church treasuries the year round. They have their reward. Live for wealth, pleasure, ambition and these wait at your door.

The writer knows a church whose leading members live for the salvation of souls as others live in the social realm or cultivate the aesthetic element and it has conversions the year round.

Twenty-one members pay the tithe through the church treasury. The church has a pure system of finance. It might be called a laymen's church. Prominent in its work, they lead prayer, class and cottage meetings and provide the temporalities. But—and it ought to be said —it is not a woman's church in the popular sense that the burden of church work falls upon over-worked women.

The type of Christianity is strong, practical and manly. The brains, hearts and hands of men lead. The women stand by them in every good work. Clear in the experience of holiness, they know how to pray and God honors faith in the salvation of souls at all seasons of the year.

The average church may constantly be a soul-saving institution.

But the kingdom must be first. Matt. 6:33.

The preacher should seek the salvation of souls in every sermon and all church work.

To lead his scholars to Christ should be the constant aim of every Sunday-school teacher.

The Gospel net should be drawn at every opportunity. The Sunday night service may be definitely evangelistic. Expect conversions and have them.

The church saying, "This one thing we do," and "all at it and always at it," brings things to pass.

To win men to Christ in season and out of season, the church must have members trained to personal work. The personal touch counts. Hand picked fruit is best.

And finally the church must receive its Pentecost if sinners are to be converted and the work of soul-saving lifted to its proper plane as the one business of God's redeemed people. "And they were all filled with the Holy Ghost.'....They were added unto them about three thousand souls.....And the Lord added unto the church daily such as should be saved.—Acts 2:4; 41, 47.

CHAPTER XXX.

PASTORAL EVANGELISM.

If the evangelistic spirit and revival fires are waning upon our church altars, may we not in part account for it by a comparison of our ministry with that of early Methodism?

THE EARLY PREACHER.

It meant much of sacrifice to be a preacher in early Methodist times. Often no church building, or parsonage, or official board to fix a salary, or Epworth League to arrange a pleasant reception for the preacher. He went forth, like Abraham, not knowing whither he went, preaching everywhere, expecting salvation at every service, the Lord confirming the Word with signs following."

A denouncer of wickedness in high places and low, he as quickly rebuked sin in the President of the United States as in the poorest sinner. He left paths to wealth and distinction, voluntarily accepting privation and poverty. The toils and exposures of the ministry might weaken his constitution and shorten his life, if violent mobs did not kill him. When the call of God was recognized and the consent of the will secured to obey, so much was involved in the choice that the man was marked among his fellows for his convictions, the extent of his life-sacrifices and the courage of his life. Such experience and training produced stalwart men, mighty men, leaders of men, whose ministry was not in word only, but in power. They spake as those having authority and not as the scribes. What was the fear or favor of man to him, who had forsaken all for Christ? Men might kill his body, but he feared God, who had power not only to kill but to cast soul and body into hell.

THE MODERN PREACHER.

The young man to-day may cast about him and ask, "What shall I choose as a life's work? The law offers opportunities of fortune and fame. I can practice medicine or engage in business, with prospects of success. But take it all in all, I will enter the ministry. I am not very strong any way. Politics is a dirty pool; the laws of trade exacting; not one merchant in a thousand finally succeeds; but the ministry in many ways is suited to my taste. It is true, I do not appreciate the itinerary; I prefer a settled home, with more of the comforts of life; but, by being careful not to offend, I may stay for years. I can have leisure for self-culture which none of the other professions afford. My associates will be churchly minds. I may not get rich, but shall be sure of a living, and with the pulpit as my throne of power may command the attention and respect of my fellow men."

LACK OF A HIGH MORAL PURPOSE.

Whatever advantage these considerations afford, they indicate lack of conviction, deep moral earnestness, and are a source of weakness and danger to the ministry and the church.

We are men of finer texture, they were of firmer mould. We are more cultured, they were more rugged. We move with the policy of statesmen through difficult and delicate surroundings,but lack the decision, the resolute bearing,the manly courage, the swing of victory of our fathers. The times have changed. We are living in a complex state of society, their life was simple. They needed physical courage to endure privations, we moral courage of a higher order to search out and condemn sin of a subtle character intrenched in high places and low.

Another reason for a lack of the evangelistic spirit and revival fires may be suggested. The pastor to-day is a man of affairs. His work is not simply preaching and evangelizing, but he is at the head of an enterprise having many departments. He must be a well equipped man. If not carrying into detail the work of the societies, he stands ready to direct the leaders of them. This broadens him. But the process results in the loss of the evangelistic gift and power. The need of the hour is pastoral evangelism. Paul's advice to Timothy, "Do the work of an evangelist," should be heeded by every pastor. Timothy was a pastor.

A call to the ministry is a call to save souls. This is his one work. Difficulties may stand in the way—church building, church debts, societies, weddings, a worldly church—but the passion for souls, which will come with the gift of the Holy Ghost, will sweep away the barriers.

If the pastor is weighted with the routine of a heavy machinery that threatens to engross and secularize him, let him cry mightily to God for deliverance, and tarry at Jerusalem until he be endued with power from on high. In answer to believing prayer, God will endow his ministers with the gift of the Holy Spirit in such measure and power as shall make them soul winners.

CHAPTER XXXI.

SPECIAL EVANGELISM.

The law of division of labor obtains in the ministry.

"He gave some, apostles; and some, evangelists; and some, pastors and teachers;

"For the perfecting of the saints, for the work of the ministry, for the edifying of the body of Christ."—(Eph. 4: 11, 12.)

It requires the whole ministry—apostles, prophets, evangelists, pastors and teachers—with the diversities of gifts, to carry forward the work of the Holy Spirit in the church and in the world.

I do not know whether the evangelist of to-day sustains exactly the same relation to the church that the evangelist did in Biblical times, but God is raising up men and women and thrusting them forth as never before into the highways and hedges; visiting the sick, the poor, the neglected, the vicious; distributing tracts, religious books, papers and Bibles; singing, pleading, praying with the individual or the mass, in country school or city church, in foreign or home field. Cultured or ignorant of letters, ordained or unordained of men, God is thrusting them out. "It is the Lord's doings, and it is marvelous in our eyes."

This is a day of specialists. One may not be master of all knowledge. Science, literature, art—each is divided into many departments. A man may give his life to the cultivation of one specialty without exhausting what may be known in his chosen field.

With the diversified tax upon brain and heart, the pastor may, without reflection upon himself, call to his aid his brother or sister, whom God may have more signally endowed with the evangelistic gift.

I would use evangelists as we use editors of religious papers, the tract, the book, the missionary, the church dedicator, or teacher of special gifts, as I had need—not to supplant, but to supplement my efforts.

CHAPTER XXXII.

FAITHFUL PREACHING.

Son of man, I have made thee a watchman unto the house of Israel: therefore hear the word at my mouth, and give them warning from me.—Ezek 3:17.

The relation between preacher and people is intimate. Dependent upon them for support and open doors he is in danger of forgetting who called him to the ministry and to whom he is responsible. The people may come to feel that the preacher belongs to them and that he must preach to please them.

CALL TO PREACH.

The call to the ministry comes from God. "No man taketh this honor unto himself, but he that is called of God, as was Aaron." The conviction is frequently so deep that the subject of it cries out, "woe is unto me if I preach not the gospel." Other callings may offer inducements but he cannot heed them. He may plead poverty, ignorance, or a stammering tongue. Unfitness and possible failure stare him in the face, but eternity is before him, perishing souls and his own salvation tremble in the balance. He is dealing with God.

Called of God with a divine message of utmost importance to sinning, dying men, the position of the minister is unique.

ANGELS NOT CHOSEN.

God might have called angels to this work, "But we

have this treasure in earthen vessels that the excellency of the power might be of God and not of men." The priests under the old covenant ministered to the people and offered sacrifice for sin. The prophets were an irregular ministry specially called of God to warn and instruct as well as tell the people what should come to pass. The priestly function has passed while the ministry which more nearly resembles the prophet's calling remains. God's charge to His prophets is His charge to His preachers today.

TO SOUND THE ALARM.

The watchman upon the walls, trumpet in hand, gave the alarm when danger threatened the peace or safety of the city.

Zion's watchman is commissioned: "Cry aloud, spare not, lift up thy voice like a trumpet, and show my people their transgressions and the house of Jacob their sin." Isa. 58:1.

When he sounds the alarm and the people take not warning, their blood is upon their own heads. But if he see the evil and utter no warning and the people perish their blood will be required at the watchman's hand. The trumpet must give no uncertain sound.

The prophet was to declare the word of the Lord fearlessly. He must "cry aloud" whether men would hear or forbear. He was not to be influenced by possible results.

NOT TO FEAR MEN.

For the Lord spake thus to me with a strong hand, and instructed me that I should not walk in the way of this people, saying,

Say ye not, a confederacy, to all them to whom this people shall say, a confederacy; neither fear ye their fear, nor be afraid.

Sanctify the Lord of hosts himself; and let him be your fear, and let him be your dread. Ezek. 8, 11, 12.

The prophet is not to walk in "the way of the people," to compromise with sin, however plausible or popular. His clear utterance of truth may cause people to withdraw their support, malign his good name, threaten or execute violence upon him. He is not to fear them but sanctify the Lord of hosts and fear Him. A wholesome fear of the Lord would straighten up many a compromising, weak kneed preacher.

DUMB DOGS.

Jewish history records the frequent falling into wickedness of priests and prophets.

Jeremiah utters a wail;

The priests said not, Where is the Lord? and they that handle the law knew me not; The pastors also transgressed against me, and the prophets prophesied by Baal, and walked after things that do not profit. Jer. 2:8.

For from the least of them even unto the greatest of them everyone is given to covetousness; and from the prophet even unto the priest everyone dealeth falsely. Jer. 2, 8, 13.

Zepheniah lifts up his voice:

His prophets are light and treacherous persons: her priests have polluted the sanctuary, they have done violence to the law. Eeph. 3. 4.

Hosea exclaims:

The watchman of Ephraim was with my God; but the

prophet is a snare of a fowler in all his ways, and hated in the house of his God. Hos. 9, 8.

A remarkable fact is brought out in connection with the falling away of the prophets:

His watchmen are blind; they are all ignorant, they are all dumb dogs, they cannot bark; sleeping, lying down, loving to slumber.

Yea, they are greedy dogs which can never have enough, and they are shepherds that cannot understand; they all look their own way, everyone for his gain, from his quarter. Isa 56-10, 11.

Why were the watchmen "dumb dogs?" Because they were "greedy dogs." They knew that the faithful prophets had fared badly, were not well fed but often stoned, hunted down like wild beasts and put to death for their exposure of wickedness in high places.

The false prophets considering prudence the better part of valor would not cry out against iniquity in a definite and fearless way so as to be felt and feared by the wicked in authority, the rich and influential. They would argue: "God does not require his servants to endanger their lives, reputations or salaries. Religion is a pleasant service. It brings peace, not strife, among men, A life of self sacrifice, the martyr spirit, are figments of heated imaginations." And thus it might be written of their tribe in all generations. They saved themselves others they could not save.

"LIKE PEOPLE LIKE PRIEST."

And there shall be, *like people like priest;* and I will punish them for their ways, and reward them their doings.

In all ages the people mold the character of the priests. The people have the kind of preachers they want or by a process of attrition tone them down to their liking. This is natural. The congregation numbers one thousand; the preacher one. The ratio of influence is as one thousand to one, in favor of the people.

But "one shall chase a thousand and two put ten thousand to flight." "One with God is a majority." Thus the great battles for God have been fought. God with Gideon, Daniel, Paul, Luther, Wesley made them invincible marching from victory to victory over sin and the hosts of Satan.

A wonderful and horrible thing is committed in the land; The prophets prophesy falsely, and the priests bear rule by their means; and *my people love to have it so*:—Jer. 53:0, 31.

False prophesying. Bearing rule by money. What corruption and what a revelation, "the people love to have it so."

LINCOLN'S BIBLE.

When Abraham Lincoln received the nomination to the presidency; he called on the ministers of Springfield, Ills., to feel the pulse of the church on the abolition of slavery. With two or three exceptions the ministers said the time is not ripe for such a movement. Slavery can not be abolished.

The attitude of the preachers greatly affected Mr. Lincoln. He paced the floor of his room in agony, saying; "I do not profess to be much of a Christian, but I do not so read my Bible." Why did these preachers with the same Bible that Mr. Lincoln had think the slavery abomination should not be swept "with the besom of destruction?"

The answer is given by the prophet, "Like people, like priest," and "the people love to have it so."

FALSE PROPHETS.

During slavery times preachers, south of the Mason and Dixon line, were generally silent on the abomination. They had open Bibles,were men of sense and the horrors of the institution were before their eyes. Why were they silent? They were "dumb dogs" because "greedy dogs." They were white slaves. The people were their masters. It was the old story. "Like people, like priest" and "the people love to have it so."

A strange Scripture is Micah 2:11 .If a man walking in the spirit and falsehood do lie, *saying,* I will prophesy unto thee of wine and of strong drink; he shall even be the prophet of this people.

IN BONDAGE TO THE SALOON.

Does the prophet mean that when the people are given to drunkenness he who, stifling convictions of right and duty, praises wine and strong drink as good creatures of God, not to be despised but rightly used, shall be the prophet of the people?

At least we have known prohibition preachers, who dared to say that "the liquor traffic can never be legalized without sin," and that men can not vote to legalize it without being partners to the iniquity, having uneasy pastorates coming to abrupt ends.

Preachers in general conferences, assemblies and associations resolve that "the liquor traffic can never be legalized without sin," but in the voting booth where they may express themselves to the government are "silent as mummies." Their votes can not be distinguished from those of brewers, distillers and saloonists, who never vote against their own interests.

Would that the *acts* of the apostles agreed with the *resolutions* of the apostles.

Are we under bondage to the liquor power as our fathers were to slavery? Is it "like people, like priest?' Is it because "the people love to have it so?"

PAUL AN EXAMPLE.

Paul was a faithful preacher. To the church at Corinth he wrote:

"I am determined not to know anything among you, save Jesus Christ, and him crucified."

Corinth was a cultivated, corrupt city. The home of artists, sculptors, poets, orators, statesmen. Paul was a man of varied attainments, but he would not know the people for their wealth or learning. One work was his. He would know Jesus Christ and him crucified.

For do I now persuade men, or God? or do I seek to please men? for if I yet pleased men, I should not be the servant of Christ. Gal 1:10.

He could not please men; if he did he was not a servant of Christ.

HE DID NOT COVET.

In the same spirit he exclaimed: "I seek not yours but you. I have coveted no man's silver or gold or apparel." The preacher who can look his congregation kindly and truly in the eye and say, "I do not covet your money. My happiness does not depend upon a large salary or a fine church. I am not dependent upon the friendship of a worldly church or the wicked rich" is a king among men compared to the poor slave in the pulpit who dare not call his life his own, his mouth beautifully closed with a golden clasp.

PAUL'S ADVICE TO TIMOTHY.

An old man in prison, with the headman's axe and the judgment seat in view, Paul instructs Timothy, and through him the ministry of all ages;

I charge thee therefore before God, and the Lord Jesus Christ, who shall judge the quick and the dead at His appearing and His kingdom.

PREACH THE WORD.

Preach the word; be instant in season, out of season; reprove, rebuke, exhort with all long suffering and doctrine.

For the time will come when they will not endure sound doctrine; but after their own lusts shall they heap to themselves teachers, having itching ears;

And they shall turn away their ears from the truth, and shall be turned unto fables.

But watch thou in all things, endure afflictions, do the work of an evangelist, make full proof of thy ministry.

"Preach the word." How the words sound through the ages. His not to make or mend, but proclaim the gospel.

HE IS TO REBUKE.

He is to 'reprove, rebuke and exhort with all long-suffering and doctrine." He was not to be squeamish but rebuke them that sin before all that others also may fear, without preferring one before another, doing nothing by partiality." A backslidden church votes such a course radical, and the preacher who should follow his discipline and the word of God as ungentlemanly if not erratic. We usually observe a prudent silence until we find something to compliment, then we ply all the arts to please and win the offender, if not to Christ, at least to ourselves.

CATERING TO THE RICH.

The early church showed a strong disposition to regard the rich and despise the poor. Jas. 2, 1-9.

The disposition still lives in the church. But if we have respect of persons we sin.

And finally this heaven-born message is to be delivered in a spirit of perfect love, without any trace of bitterness or harshness.

Let the apostle again speak and be our model.

THE LOVE OF CHRIST.

The center of his heart in all his labors and sacrifices is seen in the utterance, "The love of Christ constraineth us." Hear his solemn affirmation: "I say the truth in Christ, I lie not my conscience bearing me witness in the Holy Ghost, that I have great heaviness and continual sorrow in my heart. For I could wish that myself were accursed from Christ for my brethren, my kinsmen, according to the flesh." Roman 9:1-3.

A WEEPING MINISTRY.

His message was soaked in tears; "By the space of three years I ceased not to warn every one night and day with tears."

His love was not dependent upon the good will he received in return. He sought no selfish ends: "I will gladly spend and be spent, though the more abundantly I love you the less I be loved."

THE TRUTH IN LOVE.

"Speaking the truth in love" are words that should be engraven upon every preacher's heart. The truth may be preached of strife and envy, and love may degenerate into a soft sentimentality. But truth and love compounded by the divine alchemist in the preacher's heart are to flow from lips touched with a live coal from off God's altar.

CHAPTER XXXIII.

MINISTERIAL COURAGE.

Sin stalks over the land. Intemperance, lust, greed in business, corruption in politics and gambling prevail.

The minister in front of the battle is in an exposed position. "It is the business of a leader to lead." He must furnish enthusiasm for the rank and file of the soldiery. His position is unique.

The press may be dominated by the money power; the platform pleads its mission to entertain and instruct; the politician subordinated to the saloon hopes to lead his party "following a little in the rear."

The pulpit is said to be in bondage to the pew. "Like people like priest" is quoted to show that in all ages this tendency has existed. But the conviction is righteous that the pulpit should speak as the oracle of God. There, at least, the truth in love should be spoken without fear or favor.

Courage is needed to meet the sins of the church. Dependent upon his people for support and open doors the relation is intimate and delicate. Ministers as a class are sympathetic. They excel in the art of ministering comfort. If unappreciative of men or the refinements of life, they are unsuited to the sacred office. But strength in these directions may mean weakness in others. To rebuke sin in the man who invites you to dine with him, whose elegant family, appreciative of your ministry, knows how to pay the delicate compliment, is a problem so difficult that it is becoming a lost art.

THE MINISTER'S DEPENDENCE.

It militates against the minister's independence that he is expected to keep step with his brethren. A church with thousands of dollars in property, in which the people justly pride themselves, with social and political predilections, and grooves well worn, asks the minister not to be an iconoclast, but to deal gently with sacred records and achievements and even prejudices.

There are conventional ideas and methods of propriety, which are defined in written and unwritten code. The conventionalities which guard and strengthen may narrow and intimidate him.

MINISTERS IN EARLY TIMES.

The young man enters the ministry under different conditions from what he did a generation ago. He decided to preach then after terrible heart searching and facing difficulties of all kinds. His support was meager and uncertain. The Methodists, poor and despised, offered no temptation to seek honors or ease in the ministry. The consecration necessary to enter the sacred office was unusually deep. Cut loose from the world, he gave up hope of riches or worldly preferment. His wants were few. With such start, and the bridges burnt behind, he would not be a timid, cowering character.

The early preachers excelled in physical courage. They met wild beasts and wilder men, swam streams, slept in log cabins, preached in fields and homes of the people and were sent to communities without organized society. They were stalwarts—the material of which heroes and martyrs are made.

We study to please and excel in the art. Our gifts and

graces" are estimated by our acceptability to the people. Trained not to offend we are veritable diplomats, solving knotty problems, often by not touching them. If not born with this fine instinct and incapable of acquiring it, we cannot succeed in the pastorate.

We emphasize prudence. Is the cause politic? Will the measure win favor? Will it carry with the people? Once emphasis was on the side of courage, even wild daring for the right.

Presiding elders, dealing with young preachers, seventy-five times out of a hundred, advise prudence rather than a bold stand for the right, whatever the consequence.

The teaching in theological seminaries drills prudence into the students—a virtue which over-estimated easily descends to dastardly cowardice.

WOMAN'S MOULDING INFLUENCE.

A lack of boldness in ministers, if there be such deficiency, may be in part accounted for by their constant association with women in the conduct of the church. Women form the larger part of church members and workers. They are the majority at prayer-meeting. They prevail in number and influence as Sunday school teachers. The social functions of the church are in the hands of ladies. The pastor, the guest of honor, on these occasions is not a success if he cannot please his host. He is present at meetings of the Women's Foreign and Home Missionary societies and keeps in sympathetic touch with the Ladies Aid Society. She may form the larger part of the Sunday morning congregation.

His pastoral visiting is largely among women of the church and congregation. The men are in shops, offices and fields. Aggressive pastors visit places of business and homes after working hours and meet the men.

An evangelist was checked for frequently addressing the congregation as "dear sisters." His afternoon meetings were composed largely of ladies.

From this association the minister gains much that is valuable, almost indispensable to his character and ministry. In the society of bright and consecrated women as church workers he may acquire fineness of character, quickness of perception, grace of speech, polish of manner and withal an inspiration to be his best. He is at an advantage over the man who seldom associates with the opposite sex at its best.

But the prevailing influence amidst which he does his life's work may surcharge him with refinement rather than strength, with gentle rather than courageous life.

GIFTS MAY INFLUENCE THE PREACHER.

Gold watches, gold headed canes, rocking chairs and trips to Europe presented to popular pastors, are pleasant, but obtained at the cost of manly independence and strength of character. Judges in old Testament times were forbidden to receive gifts. They have been in all ages. Leaders are in danger of biased judgment and a doubtful stand for the right who receive gifts.

LARGE SALARIES.

If ministers must have large salaries, fine appointments and surroundings, the opportunities of culture and society for themselves and their families, they become effeminate in moral fiber. Their ministry is a campaign, not to save sinners and build up the kingdom, but to save themselves and build themselves up securely in the best positions. In a forward movement they want to be in the front—for themselves.

Jesus bearing testimony to John Baptist's character, said, "What went ye out into the wilderness to see? A reed shaken with the wind? A man clothed in soft raiment? Behold they which are gorgeously appareled and live delicately are in king's courts. But what went ye out to see? A prophet? Yea, and much more than a prophet."

No timorous, yielding character; no reed shaken with the wind, but a giant oak he stood erect in the forest. He was not clothed in soft raiment, the apparel of those who dwell in king's palaces. This goes with luxurious life. He was a man of the wilderness, robed in camel's hair, with a leather girdle about his loins eating locusts and wild honey.

If delicately surrounded and luxuriously dined, robed and housed, he would be too soft and weak a man, however kindly disposed, to herald the coming of the conquering Christ. A child of nature with few wants, he rebuked rulers of church and state, and King Herod himself for living in adultery—at the cost of his head. He was too great to be a favorite of kings or a pet of society.

This portraiture is for all times and all men. It is universally true, the more dependent the weaker; the more shielded the more delicate we are.

ORDINARY PASTORAL WORK.

The ordinary work of the pastorate requires the soldierly spirit. Pastors are sent to charges where members are living impure lives, perhaps in adultery; where drug stores, owned by church members, sell intoxicating liquors as a beverage and other members patronize them; where politicians, who are professed Christians, buy and sell votes, church members patronize Sunday railway trains, Sunday baseball, dance and attend the theatre and do things doubtful and wicked in the sight of God and man.

These people of influence and wealth have something to do with the finances, support of the ministry and the social life of the church. Their nod and beck make and unmake ministerial appointments. These conditions require the preacher to add to his faith, courage. While he prays to be wise as a serpent and harmless as a dove, he needs also to cry out for mighty courage, for Holy Ghost boldness to declare the whole counsel of God. He needs a face like flint, that fears not man, who can only kill the body, but God who can cast both soul and body into hell.

If he thinks that the better part of valor is discretion and adjourns meeting the issues, everything may go smoothly to death. With such conditions aggressive Christianity is impossible and the church really a farce.

If a pastor fears leading members living in sin and will not tell them in a spirit of love and truth wherein their lives are wrong and what they must do to be right with God and man, he cannot have a genuine revival.

It requires courage for the watchman on the walls of Zion to cry aloud and spare not, and show the people their sins and the house of Israel their iniquities. But not less to go to the individual offender without reference to his wealth and social standing, and sitting in his office, library or parlor say, "Thou art the man." This need of the hour demands a high quality of character.

True courage is not rash but is guided by wisdom. With a proper setting in humility it consists with love. One may be bold and tender. Moses, God's minister, was the meekest of men, but not the weakest.

CHAPTER XXXIV.

THE MINISTER AS A MAN.

Take heed unto thyself, and unto the doctrine; continue in them: for in doing this thou shalt both save thy self, and them that hear thee. 1 Tim. 4:16, is Paul's advice to Timothy.

The expression "take heed unto thyself" and "save thyself" are parts of the text I will emphasize. If the minister takes "heed to himself" and saves himself in a comprehensive way, his ministry will not be lost.

A GOOD ANIMAL.

Beginning at the bottom he should be a good animal A sound physical life is the basis upon which to build a noble manhood and enduring character and influence.

I am not in sympathy with the old idea that in a family of boys the weakly one, by reason of that fact, is foreordained to be a clergyman.

FRAIL BODIES.

The minister who struggles against a feeble constitution spends time and strength resisting weakness that might be employed in pushing forward the work of the gospel. Much has been accomplished by men having frail bodies, but at great sacrifice. How much more might have been done by these noble workers we know not, but a good constitution and a fair degree of health are requisites in a calling making heavy drafts upon the vital energy.

A MANLY MAN.

The minister should be a manly man. When he is ninety per cent preacher and ten per cent man he and the church suffer though neither may know the ailment.

One of his members said of a preacher; "when he goes into the pulpit I could wish he might never come out, and when he is out I wish he might never go in."

Another derisively says of the minister: there are three sexes, male, female and clergyman.

The ministry compares favorably with any class in the community. I would have him physically well equipped, superior mentally, highly endowed socially, spiritually a giant.

For a minister to break in any department of his life or work, to be blameworthy in the essentials of Christian manhood, is a fall causing universal regret.

To hear the groundlings say, "aha! there goes your preacher. There's nothing in him. I make no profession, but I am more of a man than he," brings a blush of shame to the church.

CHARACTER THE REAL THING.

Character not ordination is the real thing. He teaches by what he is. His character preaches. We need more manhood less professionalism.

A WHOLE MAN NEEDED.

The calls upon the ministry for Christian manhood are so many that Henry Ward Beecher factiously says; "When God calls very loud at the time you are born, standing at the door of life and says, "quarter of a man come forth! No; that will not do for the ministry. "Half a man come forth! No that will not do for a preacher. Whole man come! that is you. The man must be a man and a full man, that is going to be a true Christian minister, and especially in those things which are furthest removed from selfishness and the nearest in alliance with divine love."

COMMON SENSE A FACTOR.

Called to be a leader he should have a fair degree of common sense. A theological professor advised his students to select as wives those who had first, common sense, second piety, and third good health.

When asked if he had not made a mistake in placing sense before piety, he replied, "No! If she has common sense she can get piety, but if she lacks common sense nothing will supply this deficiency."

The rules for a preacher's conduct, in the Methodist discipline contain this sentence "you will need to exercise all the sense and grace you have."

Who has not found it true and often cried in his extremity, "Lord who is sufficient for these things."

SYMPATHY.

The unsympathetic man is no more called to the ministry than an elephant is called to minister to little chickens. If a cold natured man is in the ministry, and is sure that he has not answered some other man's calling let him cultivate sympathy and love for the common people.

Others may be critics and censors of men, his heart

should come close to every man's heart, so that men tempted, falling into error, whose lives are covered with shame shall find in the preacher a brother.

The miner, the quarryman should feel that his better clothes and superior culture are no barrier to their common brotherhood.

The mother in the kitchen with poverty, and a large family of children should feel sure of her pastor's sympathy in her cares, sorrows and joys.

COURAGE.

Courage is not lacking in the Christian character. We are exhorted to "add to faith, courage." I do not mean bull dog pertinacity, self will that would die rather than yield. That says "I said I would and I will or die." This has often served good purposes and ignoble uses.

I mean the higher quality of moral courage. This may consist with physical weakness and even a degree of physical fear, but it is a higher thing, as mind is above matter.

It is that which enables one to stand by his convictions, maintain the truth, overcome difficulties, stand alone and suffer and die for the truth.

SINCERITY.

The elements of truth, reality, sincerity, should be his as pure gold refined in the fire.

A Christian lady of discernment said of a minister, "He seems to be two different men."

In the pulpit he is out and out for God: In the parlor politic, conservative.

In the pulpit he allows no place for sin: Among men he hesitates,presents theological doubts,is cloudy, befogged.

In the pulpit he utters no uncertain tone; out of it he strikes no certain note. In the pulpit he is full of enthusiasm. It seems that a few such spirit-filled men would take the world for Christ. In society his conversation is trifling, his life common place, lacking depth, high motive and moral earnestness.

PROFESSIONAL ZEAL.

He does not take his ministry seriously. His zeal is professional and can be donned or doffed as he enters or makes his exit from the pulpit.

It is difficult to be true to people's real interests, to be before their faces what we are behind their backs. With them we are cordial and complimentary. Absent we riddle them, analyze their motives and lives in a way not complimentary to them nor us. Allowing that things may be said about a man that need not be said to him; that we need not always tell the whole truth it remains that that there is want of harmony, proportion, a lack of brotherliness, and sincerity.

Whatever may be true of the absent, the speaker as a Christian is a study. He does not fully understand himself, is not understood. He does not thoroughly respect himself neither is he respected. He falls short of the full measure of a Christian man.

He may say to his wife, "I am afraid I said too much about brother A. Perhaps I was prejudiced, and not thoroughly sincere. I should not like to be judged so severely. The Christian wife will reply; "Yes, dear, I thought you went too far in your criticisms. I am sure you would not have said half as much to him. If the reports are true they are damaging and as a brother you should tell A. and give him a chance to defend himself or improve."

A CAKE UNTURNED.

Considering the causes of defective character we are reminded of Ephraim who was a cake unturned; burnt on one side and raw on the other; of Balaam, the double minded man; of Saul the insincere; of Peter skulking and denying his Lord. Bishop Vincent has a friend who prays, "Lord make me real." The prayer "Lord make me clean, clear through, and clear clean through" has impressed me for years. To be real, sincere, true, loving—this is the cure.

A HOLY MAN.

The minister should be a holy man.

True repentance breaks the sinner utterly and forever with sin.

Justified he is pardoned of all actual transgression.

Regenerated the life of God is planted in his soul. As a son he is adopted into the family and given the witness of the spirit, which enables him to say, 'Abba Father.'

Sanctified he is perfected in love, made meet for the Master's use and prepared for every good work.

The minister as a man, redeemed from sin, baptized and filled with the Holy Spirit will be honest, self-sacrificing, loving; will maintain good works, make full proof of his ministry and show himself approved unto God, a workman that needeth not to be ashamed.

CHAPTER XXXV.

MINISTERIAL APPOINTMENTS.

There are station preachers and circuit preachers; $5,000 preachers and $500 preachers; those who do not aspire to an important city charge, and others who never dream of riding a circuit. The $1,500 man is "afflicted" if sent to an $800 work. And almost any preacher feels that "if a man desire the office of a bishop he desireth a good work."

"Bishop," says the committeeman, who represents his Church at Conference, "ours is a $2,000 appointment, and the brother you propose sending us is a $1,200 preacher. His class of appointments has never ranked with ours. While our people respect Brother A., think he is a good man, and propose to be loyal, they will regard it as a letting down, and, I fear, will not endure the disappointment."

A strong city Church wanted a transfer, which the bishop favored, and telegraphed the preacher asking him to accept, who answered that he did not see how he could. Another telegram from the bishop urged his acceptance. An answer that could not be misunderstood settled it: "Will go for $1,800." A large dollar-mark might be stamped upon that pulpit and preacher.

A preacher left a Church where his return would have been welcomed. Explaining to a friend the handsome increase of salary and other temporal advantages, he said: "You do not blame me for wanting to do better, do you?"

There is a necessary and right side to the classing of

preachers. The size of his family, whether he has children of school age, ready for high school or college, are proper considerations. A parsonage is not an immediate necessity to a bachelor preacher. His literary, pulpit, social, and organizing qualities, all count.

The modern church is a workshop. The Sunday-school, Epworth League, and Missionary Society are divisions of labor. Some churches represent a high grade of organization. Unless the preacher is able to direct the various departments, or at least work in intelligent sympathy with them, he will be out of harmony with all that his appointment implies. While the best is good enough for the "poorest appointment," it is necessary to the "best class of charges."

Considerations beside the fundamental one of the minister being "a good man, full of faith and the Holy Ghost," and called to preach, enter into the problem of his appointment. After classing preachers according to "the fitness of things," there are often found wrong elements working.

Class distinction begotten of pride, strife for position, unholy tempers, the use of methods that would not add character to a politician, are "flies in the apothecary's ointment that causeth it to send forth a stinking savor."

Preachers whose early ministry was in demonstration of the Spirit and of power have lost peace with God, self-respect, and the respect of all who know them, by unholy ambitions and strife for position. Backslidden in heart, their ministry is a disappointment, destitute of spirituality and power. Unless they repent, they henceforth walk in spiritual darkness amid the forms of religion, often zealous ecclesiastics, rigid ritualists, abounding in Church ceremonies. Sticklers for order, the way of the fathers, the tradition of the elders is more to them than those great spiritual verities, love, truth, faith, meekness. Having denied the Spirit, they walk after the letter, substituting the shadow for the real, the form for the spirit. They are lower men, cursed with a curse. Spiritually blind, they have ceased to know the things that make for their peace and to be true ministers to souls. He who is not willing to preach the gospel to the poorest at cross-roads or on street corners, is not worthy to preach to the rich and cultured in great cathedrals.

If Jesus Christ were a member of Conference, what would be his grade of appiontments? Would he be a city preacher or a circuit-rider? Would he be "a safe case," without regard to "the wicked Church member," who might occupy a prominent pew and a place on his Official Board? Would he stand on his rights and demand a class of work commensurate with his ability or possible long service in the Church? If he sought position, would it be the large-salaried one, or the more difficult post—the city slums, the mission field—where the neglected masses might receive the benefit of his ministry?

When our great Exemplar was on earth, "he made himself of no reputation," had no "ministerial dignity" to support, received his appointment from the Father, and "pleased not himself." He received not "honor from men," came not to be ministered unto, but to minister, and gave his life a ransom for many. In no mystical way we understand that "Christ also suffered for us, leaving us an example that we should follow his steps."

CHAPTER XXXVI.

YOUNG MEN AND THE MINISTRY.—I.

One of the bishops of the Methodist church, in reply to the question why more young men do not enter the ministry, said that a generation ago at family altars parents prayed that God would lay his hand upon their sons and call them into the ministry.

In prayer meetings, class meetings and public congregations the prayer was often heard that God would convert and anoint men to preach the gospel.

"Now," said the bishop, "We seldom hear such prayers."

On the other hand, the spirit of many leading church members is against their sons entering the ministry. If a son is converted and feels called to preach he may be advised that there are other avenues in which he may be useful and do more good than in the ministry.

The ministry is regarded by many as a hard field, without sufficient remuneration, or openings to distinguished careers. And thus young men are diverted to fields that promise wealth, honor or ease.

Jesus' words are applicable today: "The harvest truly is great but the laborers are few." "Lift up your eyes and look on the fields; for they are white already to harvest."

How shall we get laborers into the fields already white to harvest? Jesus gives authoritative answer: "Pray ye therefore the Lord of the harvest that he will send laborers into the harvest."

He does not say plead with laborers to enter the field;

offer flattering inducements, big salaries, prominent positions and easy times, free from care and danger. But, he says, "pray." He places prayer as a key into the hands of the church with which to open the treasure of heaven. He says, "pray."

Prevailing prayer is mighty work for God. It brings results. "Pray to thy Father which is in secret and thy Father which seest in secret shall reward thee openly.

Oh, that the church might fall upon her knees and call mightily upon God to lay the burden of souls upon men, anoint them with power from on high and call them into the ministry; that men might feel the burden heavily and cry out with Paul, "Woe is me, if I preach not the gospel," and with Isaiah, after a live coal from the altar had touched his lips and his iniquity was taken away and his sin purged, "Here am I, send me."

CHAPTER XXXVII.

YOUNG MEN AND THE MINISTRY.—II.

In the preceding chapter I showed that the church is failing to pray that young men may be anointed and called into the ministry as was done by our fathers in a former generation. And it is true that if we cease to pray for a thing it falls largely out of the thought and life of the church.

I desire to call attention to another fruitful source of decline of young men entering the ministry.

It is the want of an adequate support. The ministry from a financial point is not a sinecure. While some ministers receive more than some men in business and in other professions, the majority receive a meager support. Their income is less than that of the average tradesman, while their manner of life is more expensive.

From the material side the attractions are not many to enterprising young men and their friends, who consider every phase of life and especially hoist into importance material advantage.

I am aware that men should heed the call of God to go anywhere, on any errand, at any sacrifice of wealth, ease, position or even life. Nothing should stand in the way of plain duty. Men who will not preach unless coddled with fat salaries and good city appointments are unfit representatives of the meek and lowly Jesus who went about doing good, making himself of no reputation, but taking upon him the form of a servant and humbling himself he became obedient unto death, even the death of the cross.

But we have this treasure in earthen vessels. God has not called angels but men to this sacred trust—men of like passions with their brethren of the laity—men who eat, wear clothes, live in houses, read books and papers, travel, entertain their friends, care for the poor and support, with their means, the cause of God.

If the preacher's attitude is represented by entire abandonment to the work of God the layman's obligation may not be characterized by selfishness. But he will provide a proper support for his brother who ministers to him in spiritual things that he may, unembarrassed by secular cares, prosecute his high and glorious calling.

That the church does not measure up to its obligation, whatever may be true of the ministry, is one reason that young men have feared to abandon their material prospects for the work of the ministry.

For this reason the ranks of the gospel ministry have been made up from the middle and poorer walks of life and from the country.

It was true of Gentile converts, of the apostles and most of the early preachers that not many mighty, not many noble, are called:

But God hath chosen the foolish things of the world to confound the wise; and God hath chosen the weak things of the world to confound the things which are mighty;

And base things of the world, and things which are despised, hath God chosen, yea, and things which are not, to bring to naught things that are:

That no flesh should glory in his presence.

I do not think that the gospel ministry would be enriched if its candidates came from the ranks of the mighty and the noble of earth.

Perhaps coming from the people they are understood and know the people better. They are stronger and more virile than if brought up in mansions, nourished in idleness and dandled in the lap of luxury and ease. Just as the world's work is carried on largely by the great common people whom God evidently loves so well "because he made so many of them."

However, it has not been God's order to select his workmen mainly from the ranks of the worldly-wise, the rich and mighty of earth. But he has called some, for he says, "not many wise men after the flesh not many mighty, not many noble are called." So there have always been some—all ranks are represented and appealed to by the gospel.

The apostle gives the reason for God's selecting the body of his workmen from the humble of earth, "that no flesh should glory in his presence."

CHAPTER XXXVIII.

"OF NO REPUTATION."

Thousands of ministers have been at altars in the past twenty years seeking the baptism with the Holy Ghost. Thousands now are groaning for this gift.

These are intelligent seekers. Men of thought, their lives are given to meditation and prayer. The Bible is their text-book. They understand the theology of holiness, and know that they that "hunger and thirst after righteousness shall be filled."

Conscious of the call to preach, they desire the prosperity of Zion. But the base metal, mixed with the silver, mars their character and work.

Prostrate they cry for cleansing. Searching questions are flashed through their hearts by the Spirit who "searcheth all things, yea, the deep things of God."

A preacher's reputation is paramount. Without it he is worthless. With plenty of this "stock in trade" he may transfer to the ends of the earth.

Others with equal ability, learning and piety, may live without particular note, and die,

Unwept, unhonored and unsung"—

by newspapers and the popular crowds.

Carnality may emphasize itself differently in business men and society women, but his "reputation" is the tap root of a preacher's life.

Visions of consecration affecting his appointments and ambitions stagger him. This coin he counts like a miser.

The Spirit may suggest, "are you willing to preach

the gospel on street corners, in school-houses, on 'hard scrabble appointments,' as well as to the rich in cathedrals? Will you not be a place-seeker? Will you preach hell and holiness as God reveals them, without mincing before great or small? Are you willing to be misunderstood? Will you meekly endure misrepresentation? Can you stand, a man among men, to be undersized?"

Groaning under the consciousness of a divided heart, with a foe lurking within, that disturbs his peace and vitiates his strength he cries, "woe is me! for I am undone, because I am a man of unclean lips, and dwell in the midst of a people with unclean lips, for mine eyes have seen the king, the Lord of hosts."

If able to meet the tests, and say, "yes," to all the will of God, the next step, a life process, will be to "perform the doing of it."

There is a life as well as an act of consecration. And the life is all important. It has its difficulties and dangers.

One may pass the test of consecration as an act, but miscarry in the life process. His estimate of men and things change in the act of purification. God and eternity, in a real way, enter his estimates of values in the life that now is. He sees the meanest stamped with the image of God, and the greatest as grasshoppers.

Dead to the world he treats its applause and scorn as naught. But he must remember that the world is also dead to him.

Before he reckoned himself "dead indeed unto sin" he may have been influential. At least, if he did not change the current, he moved with it.

The world now looks into his face as into the face of

a corpse, and, as it passes, says with pity, perhaps scorn, "he is dead." The dead cease to be counted among the living.

Think it not strange if he no longer occupies a chief seat in the synagogues, nor is a favored leader. He may be branded a troubler of Israel; a fanatic, whose zeal outruns his judgment, a schismatist, promoting strife.

His name may be cast out as evil because with Paul he says:

"What things were gain to me, those I counted loss for Christ.

"Yea doubtless, and I count all things but loss for the excellency of the knowledge of Christ Jesus my Lord: for whom I have suffered the loss of all things, and do count them but dung, that I may win Christ.

"And be found in him, not having mine own righteousness, which is of the law, but that which is through the faith of Christ, the righteousness which is of God by faith."—Phil. 3:7-9.

How real is the life of reputation, and how real the death to sinful self.

One minister feared to consecrate all to the Lord lest he should be thrown out of the ministry and the church.

God gave him the victory over "Doubts and fears a howling wilderness."

But, as he feared, a worldly church, in a hard-fought battle, sought his downfall. While saying he was pure gold they tried to throw him onto the junk pile for old iron.

Brethren in the ministry, let us "count the cost." Reality, not sentiment counts. The battle demands earnestness. Soldiers in battle, not on parade, win victories, or die.

"Be thou faithful unto death," is the command. We are to "forsake all."

"If any man come to me, and hate not his father, and mother, and wife, and children, and brethren and sisters, yea, and his own life also, he cannot be my disciple.

"And whosoever doth not bear his cross, and come after me, cannot be my disciple."

CHAPTER XXXIX.

ONE SMALL CHURCH.

Two years in the life of one small church! They were great years; great financially; great spiritually; great in labors, conflicts and victories.

People wondered that a church paying for years on the pastor's salary one hundred and fifty-three dollars should leap to a position where twenty-five tithers, with the support of other members, pledged eight hundred dollars for pastoral support, and paid it too, with all current expenses.

They asked that they might become a station, having the entire service of a pastor, instead of being on a circuit having preaching once every two weeks—the pastor's time being divided with five other churches, having pastoral over-sight of hundreds of people scattered over territory fifteen miles square.

But how was this done? And can it be accomplished by other churches?

Back of the movement was life. A spirit of self-sacrifice must be reckoned in accounting for this work.

This spirit was shown in a sun-rise prayer-meeting, which spiritual members sustained every Sunday for years. These waited and prayed for better things, for real revival, and what they called vital Christianity. They prayed and fainted not.

One sign of God's blessing was seen at the beginning of the first year in a meeting conducted by holiness evangelists, who knew God. They prayed and "prayed through."

The burden of their message, was salvation, present, full and free. The revival was deep and true and lasting.

The best members were blessed. Young people of leading families were converted and baptized with the Spirit. The work was gracious, and a spirit of conviction pervaded the community.

After subsoiling the hearts of the church, there passed through the mind of the pastor, as by inspiration, a desire to send for a godly man of fame, for putting churches upon a sound, Scriptural, financial basis. The tithe as God's plan for financing his kingdom was presented. The members so graciously blessed needed only to see the light. Twenty-five adopted tithing, paying it into the treasury of the church. The "tithe covenent" relieved them of all other financial obligations. The church soon had money in the treasury, which was placed there without begging, festivals, tableaus, socials, or concerts. People said, "There is money in the treasury. What shall be done with it? It has not been so before. We have more than we need." Before the end of the first year the pastor's salary was paid. Still there remained money in the Lord's storehouse.

These consecrated souls, with the flush of new life, saw that they could "do exploits."

The one year and nine months of this system of church finance (the Scriptural system, as it might be called) was epochal. A rise was manifest in all departments. New life energized the work of the church. The thrill of an uplift was felt.

The prayer and testimony services were held in power; official and tithe meetings were seasons of prayer, praise and victory.

This was not what might be called a woman's church.

The women loved the church and were active in its work. But they were not overworked to raise money, often said to be "the bug-bear of the church."

The money needed was produced by men. They collected and furnished the sinewes of war.

The church was unique in being a laboring man's church. Not a rich man was active in promoting the work. With scarcely an exception every member was dependent upon day's labor.

Some churches which have greatly increased their finances through tithing, have more or less wealth. They may say that they have not, but this was undoubtedly a poor man's church. And if it accomplished these results, any church with like spirit and consecration can do great things for God.

The leaders in the movement were young people, for the most part, under thirty-five years of age.

As an element of success they made the kingdom first. When the pastor announced meetings he was not troubled to dodge counter attractions galore. The church was first; it came before business, before society, before politics, before the lodge. It *was first.* The kingdom is *first,* not second. This is God's order, and the secret of success.

This work is only possible to the deeply spiritual. It meant too much self-sacrifice to please the worldly. The spiritual work was kept in the fore. God was sought, depended upon, and honored in all the work.

The members believed in prayer. Some of them "prayed through." They were careful Bible students, and knew whether a sermon was Scriptural and uttered in the spirit. Terribly orthodox, they believed in revivals and promoted them. They knew little of higher criticism, but much of the higher life.

They were told that the church at large was watching their experiment. But it was not all "experiment;" for the word of the living God is: "Bring ye all the tithes into the storehouse, that there may be meat in my house, and prove me now herewith, saith the Lord of hosts, if I will not open you the windows of heaven and pour you out a blessing that there shall not be room enough to receive it."

It was not all "experiment;" for their pledge was redeemed. They proved the Word of God. Without resort to doubtful expedients their promise was fully met.

With shouts of victory they said these were great years, given in answer to prayer. "Behold what God hath wrought!" We give him glory, to whom all belongs.

CHAPTER XL.

THE SHEEP AMONG WOLVES.

The writer knows a church which is manned, with few exceptions, by women.

The reception given the new pastor in the parlors of the church was attended by ladies, young and old. Three married men and a few boys were the exception.

The pastor was given a surprise donation. Two of the parsonage rooms were crowded and the blessings of garden, orchard and field were heaped upon the kitchen table, but not a man, young or old, was present to share the festivities of the evening.

At the first quarterly conference the majority present were women, and they were the aggressive workers.

The Sunday-school superintendent is a woman. Five of the seven teachers are women. The attendance at Sunday-school is mostly girls and women. The majority attending church services are women.

The prayer-meeting is often held without the presence of a man, except the pastor, as the sexton is a woman.

Members of the Epworth League are young ladies and girls with an exception or two. The boys and young men are not there.

A few observations may throw light upon the situation:

1. Prominent men of the town do not regularly attend church services. They may be present in large numbers with the "orders," at funerals.

2. It is said that nearly all the men of the town drink. Some who do not go to saloons patronize drug stores. Young men of prominent families tipple. It does not seem to affect their standing in society.

3. More than forty school boys, out of one hundred and twenty, smoke cigarettes.

4. To the inquiry where are the boys and young men at the hour of Sunday-school the answer was repeatedly given "they are down on the street corners and in the saloons."

5. The women of the church, as a rule, are married to godless men. In most cases they are skeptics and free thinkers. Prominent ones are pronounced unbelievers. These godless men control the wealth and business of the town and community. In many ways they are good citizens and kind neighbors. But they are godless.

6. The unconverted husbands of these believing wives, more than is appreciated, dictate the policy of the church. If they do not directly control they affect the spirit of their wives lowering their moral tone till the wives do what will please them. They are careful not to greatly displease their husbands.

7. Christianity is at low ebb. Its character is soft and yielding. It lacks aggressiveness. It is modified. The church is not the great moral power, nor is it respected or feared as it should be.

8. Who are the girls and young women in Sunday-school, Epworth League and church to marry? In the nature of the case the boys and young men with whom they associate will become their husbands.

They will marry young men standing on street corners and tippling at grog shops and drug stores. They will marry godless and wicked men, skeptics and infidels, as "their mothers before them" have done.

Thus an effeminate church with compromised ideals of christianity will be handed down to the next generation, unless God shall mightily interpose.

OHHAPTER XLI.

BUILDING COSTLY CHURCHES.

A rage for fine churches prevails. Everywhere, in city and country, the people pride themselves on splendid temples of worship.

The condition of churches indexes the virtue and intelligence of the people. Well kept houses of worship indicate thought and care for God's cause, which is commendable.

With a million dollars to invest in benevolent enterprises, I would not place it largely in superb church edifices, but plain, substantial tabernacles for the people on frontier and in neglected districts would receive my benefactions.

If my money then needed a market, mission fields, Christian education, temperance and prohibition of the liquor traffic, holiness evangelism and slum work would be remembered.

Cities of eight thousand to fifty thousand population, with one church of their denomination, having a membership of seven hundred to fifteen hundred contemplate, when building an elegant structure, modern in architecture, costing fifty thousand to seventy-five thousand dollars, to meet "the demands of the times."

"We must keep up with the procession," they say. "Our church must not be behind sister denominations. Our city must lead neighboring cities in the display of church architecture and wealth; 'lead, never follow,' is our motto."

If fifty thousand dollars are to be expended in cities of the size named, I suggest that the amount be divided between two church structures, according to the wealth, taste and needs of the people.

I would build for the masses rather than for the classes.

The church as a rich man's club or organization destroys the very purpose for which Christ suffered and died.

Overgrown congregations need dividing. Seven hundred to twelve hundred members are too many for one pastor. Such hives should swarm. The bees will thrive better. They will make more honey.

Two churches would give two pastors work instead of one. And it means much to place a cultured, consecrated man among the people as a spiritual teacher and advisor.

The pastor of the fifty thousand dollar or seventy-five thousand dollar church would receive twenty-five hundred to four thousand dollars salary. Pastors of two churches in the same community might be paid smaller salaries, but sufficient for men intent on sacrificing all for Jesus and his church.

Their support and manner of living would bring the pastors into sympathy with working people, the mass of whom do not receive large incomes. And the common people need to feel the heart throb of the pastor in their struggle to maintain and educate their families if he is to win them to Christ and influence them for righteousness.

Two churches in different parts of the city would accommodate the people better than one possibly could.

Two churches would double the official members looking after the interests of the church in that community. The number of Sunday-school teachers, Epworth League or Christian Endeavor workers, Woman's Foreign Missionary Societies and all church workers, if not doubled, in actual count, would be increased in number and efficiency.

Two difficulties are in the way of building two plainer churches where one costly edifice is contemplated:

The ambition of ministers who would build a monument to themselves at the same time that they build a temple to the glory of God.

And wealthy official boards and congregations who would display money and style to outdo rival churches and other communities.

The above suggestions do not contain "the whole truth and nothing but the truth," but they embody truth in large enough proportions to cause reflective minds to take the sober second thought before lavishing consecrated money on great cathedral piles while the unchurched masses of our own land and the heathen by the millions perish for the bread of life.

CHAPTER XLII.

DECADENCE OF THE COUNTRY CHURCH.

Travelling through rural districts we pass neighborhoods where once were flourishing churches. Older citizens tell of strong societies in early days, of large congregations and powerful revivals.

Leading families were constant in attendance and support of the church.

NEGLECTED CHURCHES.

Those families are dead or scattered. Their children have moved to the West, or if occupying the home farm, may not be interested in the church. In many cases foreigners own the farms and never darken the doors of the church, except on funeral occasions.

If the society lives, it is but a shadow of its former self. So that the "fathers" look upon it like the Jews under Zerubbabel, who mourned when they compared their temple with Solomon's, which surpassed their own in grandeur and magnificence.

Many members upon whom the burden of the church falls are working and hoping and waiting for a change. But "hope deferred maketh the heart sick."

TWO DOZEN PEOPLE.

Country ministers preaching to two or three dozen people every other Sunday feel the situation as others cannot. The outlook is discouraging, but seeing no remedy, by a law of necessity, they continue the old way.

It might be said that conditions affecting the country church operate also upon the district school. Many of those once having large attendance are reduced to a handful. The district school is up for settlement. Educators are solving the difficulty by transporting the children to adjacent towns, or to central places in the townships.

I do not mean that in the aggregate there is less attendance and support of the cause of religion. The Methodist Episcopal church is building two churches a day every day in the year. This is largely in the West and South. Other denominations are growing at a rapid rate. The membership and attendance upon church services are in excess of what it was in a former day. The churches are doing great work at home, and Christianity is going out to the ends of the earth.

But I am speaking of conditions in rural districts of Indiana, and I am persuaded that these conditions exist in older communities outside of our state.

THE CAUSE.

To the extent that this is true it will be interesting to inquire the cause;

The general condition of society is to be considered.

People live in towns and cities more than they did formerly. At the beginning of the past century one twenty-fifth of the population lived in cities; now, more than one fifth of the people are massed in cities. It is common to find towns largely made up of farmers and their families. They are properly called country towns. And the citizens derive their living mainly from the proceeds of their farms.

The writer knows a stretch of country adjacent to an inland city, eight to twelve miles in extent where, few farms are occupied by the owners. Renters live on them. These stay a year or two. The owners may support churches in towns and cities where they live, but they do not generally support them in the vicinity of their farms. The renters, with few exceptions, do not permanently help the church, because their life in any commmunity is short and uncertain. The country church is not built up by an itinerant population, nor by absent landlords. So, between the two classes the country church suffers with a trouble that did not affect it greatly in the earlier days.

MEANS OF TRAVEL.

Fifty years ago the country was largely unimproved. Turnpikes and bridges were rare. Creeks had to be forded. Hills and hollows were a formidable difficulty. Roadways were not opened up as they are now.

Behold the change! In an era of road making and bridge building turnpikes are being constructed at a rapid rate. The facilities for travel are increased. Thirty and forty years ago buggies were a luxury. People traveled on horse back and in wagons. Every farmer is now supposed to have one or more buggies or carriages. The foot traveller is generally a tramp, and the man on horse back is rarely met.

In the last two decades the bicycle made strides into popular favor, threatening to turn the horse out to pasture as a useless luxury.

The automobile peeps up in the hands of the wealthy, with possibilities not known, but it will need to come down from the pedestal of fancy prices before it can be a popular mode of conveyance.

And interurban lines of cars are opening up cheap and rapid carriage not dreamed of in the days of our fathers. So that many of the out-of-the-way villages in the state are crying out: "We don't see why we can't have a trolley line."

These lines, connecting villages and towns, place farmers within reach of county seats and adjacent cities at rates and speed as a money and time saver.

What has this to do with the country church? Much every way, by putting rural districts in close proximity with centers of population. People leave the country for the attractions of crowded resorts, whether to attend church, the horse race, base-ball or theater, it matters not.

Five or ten miles on splendid roads is small matter, to the young fellow with fleet horse, rubber tire and his best girl. And this works against the country church.

SUNDAY DESECRATION.

Sunday desecration comes in for consideration as a militating influence against country, as well as city church.

Buggy riding, bicycling, fishing, hunting, base-ball and railway excursions on Sunday affect unfavorably churches, whether urban or suburban.

Again, in the days of which we speak, the church was the center of interest in the community. It was the commanding influence.

MANY COMPETITORS.

There are now many competitors for the time, money and energy of the people. Lodges, of all kinds have sprung up like grasshoppers in a meadow on a June morning. The women, too, are said to be "lodged to sleep, and clubbed to death." And the church suffers.

Besides, in that day, a church here and there in the country, with occasional preaching drew the people for miles. Now, church buildings distributed through the country have in them some kind of religious service every Sunday. Everywhere towns and villages have sprung up in the past generation, each of which has one or more church buildings.

While more people attend church now they are divided among multiplied congregations.

Aside from its chief function, religion, the rural church is an inspiration to all right living. It furnishes highest ideals and best society, and is one place where rich and poor may meet as equals.

What a happy meeting place! The hand shakings and kindly greetings, as the people linger around the sacred spot are sweet in realization and precious in memory.

Here the babes are christened, the young are married, and from its altars the dead are buried. It is the place of new hopes, new aspirations and new resolves; of comfort for the sorrowing, succor for the tempted, forgiveness for the sinner and character building for the Christian.

The farmer cannot afford to neglect an institution that fosters every interest dear to him, his family and the community.

And preachers should be careful how they drop country appointments because they may be distant and difficult to reach, or the people poor, lacking culture or interest, for the destiny of souls waits on their ministry in these places. Converts made and nourished in these more neglected and uninviting fields may become stars of the first magnitude in the Kingdom of our God.

CHAPTER XLIII.

A REMEDY FOR THE STARVING COUNTRY CHURCH.

In the past thirty years thousands of country churches have gone out of existence and other thousands are living at a "poor dying rate." They find it difficult to support ministers, gather congregations, pay expenses and sustain an interest in the work.

But he is a poor physician who diagnoses his patient's disease and fails to give remedies to heal his maladies. I am not brave enough to think that I can turn the tide that has set in against country churches, but trust to offer suggestions which will stimulate the weak and starving.

SPIRIT-FILLED PREACHERS.

Spirit-filled ministers who will go anywhere without regard to money, position or ease; men who hear the voice of God and obey, are needed for the more difficult fields.

This is asking much of men who have forsaken all secular employments and invested their lives, their fortunes and their sacred honor in the ministry. But less will not suffice. It is the purchasing power of self-sacrifice that wins.

He who would save others cannot save himself.

Men without the baptism of the Holy Spirit may fill easy appointments, get large salaries and do showy work, but the harder, more disagreeable labor, unsung, unhonored and unknown, requires men who have made a true consecration to God.

THE SPIRIT OF SELF SACRIFICE.

To be underpaid and overworked; underestimated and misunderstood all for the glory of God and the good of the church, is a sacrifice that men are usually not willing to make. But it is necessary to the best work.

John Wesley said if he had a hundred men who feared nothing but sin he could take England for Christ. The writer knows an evangelist who feels called to formal and dead churches. And God blesses her ministry in resurrecting many to a lively hope.

A father giving his son to the ministry preferred him to preach on circuits because he believed that work was more needed there—than more good could be done in neglected country districts than in city fields. This was an unusual consecration.

Many mothers are willing to dedicate their babes to the ministry but it is generally understood that they want them to become bishops, general secretaries or some great dignitaries in the church of God. They do not want them to be slum workers, salvation army officers, holiness preachers, evangelists or missionaries to darkest Africa.

Young men of inexperience commence their ministry in the country and old men, practically superannuated, end their ministry at the country appointment.

This plan will not build up country churches. Strong men physically, mentally and spiritually; men of experience, sound judgment and strong bodies will command respect for their message and the work.

WOLVES WITH THE SHEEP.

The writer acknowledges his obligation to the church. Through it he was converted, received Christian training, was called to the mininstry and has been given a field of work.

He recognizes in the church the salt of the earth, the light of the world. Saints in all ages have come from her altars. Reforms that have blessed the world have sprung from her loins.

But we must not be blind and deaf, nor dumb. Sinners are in the fold.

Goats are with the sheep; wolves are in the flock; tares are in the wheat.

This condition is not to be left for enemies of the church to scoff at. Its friends who mourn, must recognize and remedy the evil.

UNREGENERATE MEMBERS.

A mass of unregenerate members is the fly in the apothecary's vessel that cause the ointment to send forth a stinking savor.

Many members never attend the services of the church; they pay nothing to its support; they desecrate the Sabbath, drink, play cards, dance, attend theater, swear, visit "bawdy houses." They will not stand and be counted as Christians. They deny that they are Christians, but swear that they are church members.

TALK AND ACT LIKE SINNERS.

They talk like sinners, act like sinners, live like sinners, and, unless they repent and believe the gospel, they will die like sinners and receive the sinner's doom.

To treat them as regenerated people only needing to

grow in grace and be a little more faithful, is to do them injustice and minister to them falsely.

Their need is regeneration. This accomplished they will love the church, support its services and live right lives. The baptism with the Holy Spirit will do for the laity exactly what it will do for the ministry. It will set them going for God; cause them to be God-centered, not self-centered. The multitudes need waking up and undeceiving.

At a quarterly conference a presiding elder was in the presence of the proposition of supporting the church. The officials, well-to-do farmers, complained that their members were moving to the city; the aged were dying; the young men in the neighborhood, reckless of morals, neglected the church and were a menace to its peace and prosperity; the pastor did not visit the people sufficiently to get acquainted with the young, and in consequence of many adverse influences, the church was gradually "going down." And they were discouraged.

METHODS OF FORTY YEARS AGO.

The presiding elder said that they had given him an opportunity to say some things that had weighed heavily on his heart. The church is trying to do the work with the methods and equipment of forty years ago. The world, on the other hand, offers ten times the attractions to a life of pleasure and vice that it did a generation ago. The loud call to the church is, "go forward." "The children of this world are in their generation wiser than the children of light." A pastor having six appointments, preaching three times every Sunday, traveling fifteen to twenty miles to fill appointments, cannot meet the demands of the work.

With territory extending eight to twelve miles square containing hundreds of people it is physically impossible to do justice to the church or himself. It is the equipment of forty years ago attempting to meet present-day demands.

A farmer might as well farm with the implements of forty years ago and expect to keep pace with the up-to-date farmer as the church to work with old-time methods.

PUT MORE MONEY INTO THE WORK.

If members will put more money into the work and give the pastor fewer appointments he can give pastoral oversight, get acquainted with the young, know the people intimately, and look after the interests of the kingdom. This will mean much in every way. The church will feel the throb of life flowing through every vein.

The presiding elder touched a vital spot when he recommended country members to put more money into their church plant. Here, let it be said, softly, they fail. After a pastorate of twenty-seven years in city and country charges, and hearing from other ministers, I am free to say that farmers attempt to support the church on too economical a scale. They expect too much for the money they invest in the enterprise. Country churches are not as liberal as city churches. They do not pay in proportion to their ability as members of city charges. Farmers with one or two hundred acres of land worth five thousand to twenty thousand dollars will over and over again not pay more money into the church than mechanics, clerks, or bookkeepers, with nothing but their week's wages. They are proverbially slow in supporting the missionary cause.

COUNTRY HOSPITALITY.

The writer wishes to bear testimony to the hospitality as a pastor, he has received in country homes. But farmers are slow as compared with their city counsins in paying to support God's house. And the "sinews of war" are necessary to make the work go. Covetousness is idolatry. Let it be sounded out. We need a wide-spread revival that will open men's pocket-books. This writer can never believe that a man's heart is open toward God when his pocketbook is closed toward his church.

CHAPTER XLIV.

WORLDLINESS.

Love not the world.—1 John 2:15-17.

The epistle of John was written to correct abuses into which the church had fallen. Laxity of faith and practice prevailed. Some taught that one could love God and hate his brother! walk in darkness and be a child of the light; practice abominable wickedness and be pure and holy.

If this epistle were printed in leaded type in one of our great dailies the people would say that the religious editor had taken pen in hand to portray the condition of the modern church and utter a clarion note of warning against the flood of worldliness that inundates Zion.

1. We are not forbidden to love nature. The trees, flowers, rivers, mountains, oceans are God's handiwork. They speak of love, wisdom, power. "The heavens declare the glory of God and the firmament showeth his handiwork. Day unto day uttereth speech and night unto night showeth knowledge."

We are to love our children. They are God-given. Our brother man is created in God's image. Even our enemies are to be loved as a test of our love to God.

"We are to love in due degree the enjoyments which God has provided for our rational natures. But we are not to choose these as our portion or delight in them as our chief good. He does not say leave the world, but love not the world; he does not say use not the world, but love it not; that is seek not after the world inordinately and delight not in it immoderately. Seek it we may, but not in an undue manner; delight in it we may but not in an undue measure."

II. Consider how the spirit of worldliness is manifested.

1. —In the pulpit.

2.—In the pew.

1. The thought prevails that the minister can easily turn his back upon the subtle attractions of evil in the world.

"Is he not called of God to preach? Is he not ordained, and has he not left the world? And isn't he naturally spiritual? Temptations to him are scarcely real, and easily overcome, because he is a minister."

It is scarcely necessary to say that this shallow thinking is by people not morally earnest, working out the problem of their own destiny.

The minister's temptations are modified by his relation to life. The physician, banker, lawyer, day-laborer, preacher have temptations in common, but each meets life from his angle. Every man will be tested to the measure of his ability and will stand only as he has God in him.

A WORLDING IN THE PULPIT.

If the minister seeks the praise of men more than the praise of God; if he pleases the worldly and influential, catering to their peculiarities, touching lightly their sins, prophesying smooth things; healing the hurt of the daughter of my people slightly, saying "peace, peace," when there is no peace, he is a worldling in the pulpit.

Such a character is influenced by the spirit of the world. His pulpit does not make him spiritual, nor will it save him from the hell that awaits the hypocrite.

When he goes to the judgment seat of Christ saying, "Lord, Lord have I not prophesied in thy name and in thy name done wonderful works?" He will be answered, "I never knew you: depart from me, ye that work iniquity."

Preaching secular sermons, science, literature, art—subjects that belong to the school, the platform and the magazine, rather than the Word of God—indicate that he is secular and not spiritual.

If he makes everything bow to "success," position and personal popularity, it is a cloak of covetousness. He is an hireling and loves the world and the things that are in the world. "The love of the Father is not in him."

To such a ministry apply the words: "Woe unto you when all men shall speak well of you! for so said their fathers to the false prophets." "How can ye believe which receive honor one of another, and seek not the honor that cometh from God only?"

III. How the spirit of worldliness is manifested in the pew.

1. Worldly Conversation.

Conversation reveals character. "Out of the abundance of the heart the mouth speaketh." "They that fear the Lord spake often one to another; and the Lord hearkened, and heard it, and a book of remembrance was written before him for them that feared the Lord, and that thought upon his name."

Personal religion, treated as too sacred to be spoken of, is relegated to the church and the ministry. If our conversation is always of the world it is an index finger that points to our true characters as worldlings.

2. The Amusement Question.

The theater, card party, parlor dance, public ball, horse

race, circus, wine party, etc., are questions that appear in some form from age to age in every land. At the Iriquois theater fire in Chicago two Methodist preachers and one prominent layman were killed. Let not the names of the ministers be mentioned. For reasons known to themselves they placed their example on the side of an institution unfavorable to the spiritual life. May their influence die with them. The layman, prominent in business and church circles, was abundant in good works, and said to be a consecrated Christian. We may not judge. But Christian people everywhere deplore the occasion of his death.

These questionable entertainments have life in them. They furnish amusement for the race. They appeal powerfully to human nature, and to the baser elements in human nature.

DOUBTFUL*!* DOUBTFUL*!!* DOUBTFUL*!!!*

Efforts to harmonize them with Christianity and harness them to work side by side with the church have proven futile. The church stands for one thing and these amusements for another. The best that can be said, putting them all together, is they are doubtful. And the Christian has a right to be on the unquestionable side of every questionable subject.

3. The Church Social, Literary and Concert.

The church social, literary, fair, bazaar, festival and concert are a modern department of church work introduced to furnish pleasure, save young people to the church and replenish depleted church treasuries.

They are often popular and appear to be successful. They, at least, present the semblance of life.

In many places these entertainments have "run their day," and Christian women object to them, as being wasteful of precious time and strength, full of annoyance, out of harmony with a consecrated Christian life and best ideas of what constitutes true church work.

When the love of the social prevails over the meeting of prayer, praise and the singing of Psalms, hymns and spiritual songs we may seriously question whether we are in the love of God.

If you have a taste for concert and bazaar and a distaste for worship you are governed by "the lust of the flesh, the lust of the eyes and the pride of life," which are not of the Father but are of this world. It is the spirit of this world.

CHURCH ENTERTAINMENTS A FAILURE.

An unconverted, covetous person can serve at oyster supper or church fair and be unconverted, and wicked still. But he cannot sing the songs of the redeemed. He has no heart for prayer and testimony. Spiritual worship is only possible to the nature transformed by grace. And this is the heart of true church life.

The church entertainment fails at two points.

1. It requires the church to provide amusement for the people. And God has not called the church to cater to the amusement loving public. It has more serious business.

The entertainment is a poor advertisement of the delights of God's house and the joys of religion.

GOD'S PLAN AND OUR WAY.

2. It is a substitute for God's plan of finance. The word says: the tithe is the Lord's. Human selfishness says, "we don't want to pay it. We can't afford so much. We

might as well get the money to support the house of God out of any body and every body who will pay it, and have a good time besides. So let music and mirth go on, eat, drink and be merry; it is in a good cause, and the end justifies the means. We can entertain the public and pay our church obligations at the same time."

God says, "Ye have made the house of prayer a place of merchandise and a den of thieves."

The shrewd professor with mercenary eye replies, "Oh, well, the people want amusement, and we might as well give it to them and make them pay for it."

God says, "Ye have robbed me, this whole nation, in not paying tithes and offerings into my treasury." And the modern church replies, "We don't see it that way, but think a better plan is, let each give as he feels able, and get everybody in the community interested in some popular entertainment to pay deficiencies."

Substituting our way for God's plan, we have "forsaken the fountain of living waters, and hewed out cisterns, broken cisterns, that can hold no water." And behold the condition of the church. Her treasuries everywhere empty, and the church posing before the community as a beggar. And an Amazon of worldliness flooding Zion. Oh, when shall we learn that if we bring the tithes into the storehouse, that there will be meat in God's house and that He will open the windows of heaven and pour out a blessing that there will not be room enough to receive.

4. Business and Religion.

How does the professor of religion conduct business? Does he follow the practices and principles of the world, or is he governed by the word of God? How is his capital invested? Does he own stock in railroads or newspapers or other enterprises that violate the Sabbath day?

Does he use his property as a place upon which to manufacture or sell intoxicating liquors?

Stewards of the grace of God, we shall be held to strict account for the way in which we do business and the use of money and property entrusted to our care. The consecration of business talent is a serious problem confronting professors of religion.

Some are called to preach, others to business, and all to a life of holiness. One preaches for God, another does business for God. There are not two codes of morals, one for preachers the other for laymen.

THE LIQUOR TRAFFIC.

A Methodist is forbidden by his discipline to rent his property as a distillery, brewery, saloon or drug store, if used as a saloon. If he argues the custom of society, the competition of business and the need of money he is a sinner, and unworthy, whatever his profession.

The attitude of the church on the saloon question is a marvel of inconsistency. It is an effort to unite good and evil; to unite in holy wedlock the Son of God and the devil; to harmonize heaven and hell.

WE SAY AND DO NOT.

It is true that we say, "It can never be legalized without sin." But we say and do not. We legalize it. The vast majority of professing Christians vote in such a way that brewers, distillers and the army of saloon keepers need feel no fear nor register an objection. Indeed a majority of the preachers' ballots cannot be distinguished from those cast by gentleman behind the bar wearing white aprons. Their votes lie side by side, in the ballot box, like twin brothers.

This, our shame and weakness, is also our crime. It is our way of tearing down with one hand what we build with the other.

With power to put down the greatest organized evil of the twentieth century we perpetuate it. Think of it; less than five per cent. of professing Christians voting directly against this gigantic iniquity—the enemy of God and man. Shame on the church.

5. Secret Societies.

I do not question the right of the lodge to exist but speak of its relation to the church. People may band themselves together for social enjoyment and mutual improvement. These societies have many excellent qualities and many excellent people are connected with them, even great names in church and state. Much of their work is founded on the Bible.

But the lodge, in places, practically takes the place of the church. It has become a people's church. A human religion is substituted for the divine religion of our Lord Jesus Christ. This is the evil.

Many people, and church members, too, do not hesitate to say "the Lodge is good enough church for me."

Churches, the country over, are struggling with a handful of members attending prayer-meeting, another handful at preaching services, a small minority bearing the burdens of the church, with an empty treasury, a general lack of interest and the whole work a drag.

The same communities furnish lodges of all kinds, patronized by church members who attend one or more of their services every week but neglect the prayer meeting. They work for the lodge but have no heart for the church for which Jesus Christ gave His life's blood. They pay lodge dues, but complain and in many cases, fail to meet church obligations. And the poor church struggles and suffers and starves to death under unkind treatment of professed friends.

And members who neglect church altars and vows look wistfully at God's ministers saying: "Why don't people go to the prayer-meeting? Why is not the church crowded? Why is it so hard to support ministers and missionaries? Why don't you revive the church?"

The answer, in part, is because multitudes of professors of religion untrue to God have broken their church vows. They have forsaken the altars of God's house and allowed another institution to take its place. Their time, energy, money, influence and love are given to another and the church suffers and dies of neglect.

"Awake, awake; put on thy strength, O Zion; put on thy beautiful garments, O Jerusalem."—Isa. 52:1.

6. Worldliness a Spirit.

There are those who do not patronize forbidden amusements. Circumstances or the set they move in may prevent their enjoyment. But if we have the spirit of these we have the love of the world.

One may have a distaste for worldly amusements and vote them foolish and costly. He may also object to God's house saying its services are wearisome and expensive. Living for the world our lives may be hard. We may be greedy of gain, sensual, devilish.

The forbidden world has subtle attractions for poor fallen human nature. Her influence is insinuating, lowering ideals, setting low standards of judgment and life.

"Life may not mean pursuing worldly pleasures or mixing with worldly sets but a subtler thing than that—

a silent deference to worldly opinion—an almost unconscious lowering of religious tone to the level of the worldly religious world around.' '

THE UNIVERSITY MAY MAKE INFIDELS.

A single illustration will show the influences at work which lower the moral tone of the church. A youth is sent from a pious home to the university. The professors may be skeptical, or nominal members of the church. They are cultured men, of dignity and standing in the community. Their morals may be unexceptionable. But religion has no place in their thought or life.

The youth imbibes the spirit of his professors and the school. He soon loses religious fervor, perhaps becomes ashamed of his religious profession. After a term of years he returns home cultured, ambitious, worldly if not infidel and wicked. He may remain in the church but without power, aggressiveness, peace.

IV. Why we are not to love the world.

"If any man love the world, the love of the Father is not in him. For all that is in the world, the lust of the flesh, and the lust of the eyes, and the pride of life is not of the Father, but is of the world. And the world passeth away and the lust thereof; but he that doeth the will of God abideth forever."

"The lust of the flesh" is sensual and impure. Uncleanness, the love of strong drink, tobacco and other narcotics; is a "lust of the flesh."

Gluttony may ruin soul and body as well as intoxicating drinks.

To live from the standpoint of the animal nature is to live a fleshly, animal life.

"The lust of the eyes" is a love of finery, style, display. This is manifest in patterning after the fashions of the day in dress, fine houses, costly furniture and general style of living. The desire to get all we see; the greed for wealth is "lust of the eyes."

"The pride of life" is the desire for honors, titles, position among men; boasting of one's family connection or acquaintance with eminent people springs from the root, "pride of life."

These are not of the Father but are of the world. The world passeth away and the lust thereof but he that doeth the will of God abideth forever. This world will not always stand. "Transient" is written upon everything earthly. Sun, moon and stars shall fade and the earth pass away.

"But he that doeth the will of God abideth forever." Notice, it is not he that thinketh or talketh but he that doeth the will of God that shall abide forever. What we are last; what we do for God never fails.

This is encouragement for the child of God. He may suffer, be misunderstood, misrepresented, or underestimated by men but he is precious in God's sight.

This transient life does not span his existence. He shall live forever.

Child of God, wipe away your tears. Your sorrows shall cease with time and your joys eternal begin. Rejoice, rejoice for great is your reward in heaven.

CHAPTER XLV.

HOLINESS AND THE CHURCH.

(A letter to the Christian Advocate.)

The fear to come out definitely on the side of Wesleyan holiness, lest some prominent advocate of the doctrine and experience should "within six weeks" disgrace himself and the doctrine "is common to man."

A few years ago an advocate of entire sanctification fell. His confession was published in the "Advocates" and holiness papers; he surrendered his ministerial credentials and his family forgave him. For days he wept and agonized. His repentance seemed genuine. Learning this, I wrote him, letting him know that, as a brother preacher, I forgave him, and should still be glad to hear him preach and read his books. I forgave him as we all forgive King David—Psa. 51. I urged him to go forward, all for God, without fear of man or consequences, assuring him that, while cherished fields of influence might close to him, others would providentially open.

I do not recommend, when a minister in the maturity of his powers grievously falls, that the stamp of the Church be again placed upon him. There might be a weak place, if not a sinful spot, in his character that would render him a dangerous man. He might break again, and again appear equally sorry.

The disciplining of holiness evangelists is simply a question of exercising discipline. The evangelist who is an ordained minister is amenable to his Annual Conference, if that means anything. The evangelist who is a layman is answerable to his Quarterly Conference. Evangelists of other denominations are answerable to their own churches.

Holiness associations have no power of discipline, any more than the Woman's Foreign Missionary Society, in the church. The National Holiness Association may drop a member's name, cease to countenance him at camp meetings, and refuse to publish his articles in holiness papers under their more immediate supervision. That is as far as they may go. If more is needed, the Church is the mother of us all.

I recently heard a prominent holiness evangelist of the South in Indianapolis speak in the power of the Spirit. Preaching in the power of the Holy Spirit is a wonderful discipline of the Church. Sour holiness professors, come-outers, or evil-doers, however prominent, could extract no comfort from the heart-searching preaching. If such preaching were heard from every pulpit it would do much to cleanse the Church—I might say it would cleanse the Church.

I suggest, with reference to the possible misdemeanor of recognized leaders in the holiness movement, that one who stands for distinctive holiness is liable to be distasteful to his brethren who are indifferent or "holiness fighters." If living in sin, they will hate the white light of holiness and the standard-bearer of it. They can scarcely do such a one justice. They magnify his faults and minify his virtues, and

"Trifles light as air
Are to the jealous confirmations strong
As proofs of holy writ."

The man who retains the spirit of self-crucifixion will be true to God, as the needle to the pole. When he knows the right he will not deflect from it to save his life, or anyone else's life. A true holiness man is no ordinary man, whatever his rank in life. He is no "namby-pamby" character. He cannot have a putty face and retain holiness. If everybody's man he is not God's man. This kind of man is sure to meet strong, self-willed men, and he may find them in the ministry. He will then need to pray to be delivered "from unreasonable and ungodly men, for all men have not faith."

I have listened to many evangelists in the holiness ranks, and am convinced that the spirit of the prophets, apostles, and martyrs is restored to the Church in their ministry as it is not in any other class of our ministry. Among our truest ministers, they make sacrifices, give up home comforts, and get comparatively small compensation. This is also true of holiness pastors. If they are tempted to narrowness and criticalness, on account of the state of the Church, and the treatment they receive I regret it.

I observe with concern the "come-outism" spirit on the part of some people and preachers professing holiness. It is a mistaken spirit. If one is put out of the Church for being true to God, that is different from voluntarily going out.

Poor, ignorant, untrained souls come into the experience of holiness, or think they do. Not understanding themselves, and not being understood by semispiritual pastors and worldly churches, without sense and grace (backbone) to endure afflictions, they shrink, whine, strike back, and, falling into the hands of irresponsible leaders, who preach our glorious doctrine mixed with error, are led out of the Church, side-tracked, and often ruined. They really lack true holiness or staying power or training, one or all.

This means that our pastors should master our doctrines and, filled with the Spirit, feed the flock of Christ over which the Holy Ghost has made us overseers.

CHAPTER XLVI.

EXERCISING CHURCH DISCIPLINE.

He was an offender who drank a great deal of free beer and whiskey and used his influence openly to defeat law and order. A formidable enemy of law enforcement, for revenue, this member was really the church's worst foe and the saloon's best friend.

At a meeting this man's influence was considered, as he always had to be reckoned with. As if patience had ceased to be a virtue, one of his brother members said: "I move that we put Brother Blank out of the church." "I second the motion," was heard all over the room. "Yes," said the pastor, with emotion, "he is a menace and I have thought that something should be done."

A wise-acre, with a significant nod and grin, said, "The wheat and tares, you know, must grow together. In getting rid of the tares you might destroy the wheat. It would effect more than one. It would break the heart of his aged mother. Besides others walk disorderly and will not be reproved. You had better be careful and go slow." And he looked very knowing.

"Yes, but this member is a chief offender," said an indignant brother; "he is pronounced, and don't care for anybody or anything. He is known by saint and sinner as a dangerous foe. He is injuring the church, and would ruin it if necessary to accomplish his ambitious designs. What does church membership amount to any how?"

"Ah, yes," said the wise-acre, "but I have lived here

many years and know the people. A good many are interested and looking on, and you had better look out. The wheat and the tares, you know, must grow together." And with a twinkle in his eye, he spoke like one who knew, and would have the last word.

And I believe that a majority of the church would have thought that he uttered a wise sentence. Perhaps he did, if we are not to disturb the condition of the church as it exists.

However, the question of the professor's church membership was quietly dropped as one of the evils that must be borne with. And the faithful few took up again their burden, made heavier by the dead weight of one who had promised to be true to the Christ and his church.

The parable of the wheat and tares has served all sorts of doubtful ends. It has been the excuse for indecision and cowardly prudence. It has blinded the eye so that evil has been called good and the crooked straight. Under the name of sweet charity, wild beasts and poisonous reptiles shelter and pasture with the flock.

But what is to be done with members who hinder the work of God, whose unrighteous lives are a stigma to the cause which they should honor?

The writer knows a pastor who does not cleanse church records of the unworthy. He usually stops short of the final act. He exercises discipline in another way.

He preaches the Word, reproves, rebukes and exhorts with all long-suffering and doctrine. No person or condition may close his mouth. He speaks on social purity, though members and prominent people in the community may be living in adultery. He declares for Sunday observance, though many in his church may witness Sunday base-ball and use Sunday trains. He is out and out for temperance and prohibition, though official and other members may drink and vote to license rum .

The church may raise money by fairs, festivals, bazaars and doubtful, unscriptural schemes, the product of cunning and covetous hearts. He advocates clean church finance and declares for, at least, the tithe of every man's income to support God's cause.

Dancing, card playing, theater-going professors may look with shallow impudence into his face, ignore their vows and trample upon the discipline of their church. He fails not to lift up the voice of warning against the seductive influence of these leading worldly amusements.

Unrighteousness may prevail, but he unfurls the banner of holiness unto the Lord, without which no man shall see the Lord, as the standard of Christian living.

In addition to all this, he goes in a spirit of prayer to derelict members privately and talks with them on the condition of their souls and the influence of their lives upon their families, the church and the community.

I have known him to talk with a tobacco using local preacher, who neglected the means of grace and was found at the hour of prayer service reading the newspaper, smoking and loafing with young men. He has refused to recommend the renewal of such man's license to preach. He has secured removals from the position of teacher or church official those whose lives and influence were feared.

He talks with all classes of ungodly and wicked professors in their offices and prays with them in their homes. And looking straight into their eyes they feel, "Thou art the man." But there he stops. He usually does not take steps to put out of the church sinners who grade all the way from indifferent to openly immoral.

In justification of his course he says that the members have built the local church and largely made it as an organization. They support it. Socially, financially and morally they give it their influence. They and their families and friends may have been members of the church for years and generations. As an organization it is theirs more than his. And he respects their rights. He scarcely feels that it is proper for him to say, "You get out of here," though by their fruits he may know that they are not worthy members.

"But there is a limit to their rights. Official and influential members may not control my ministry. They do not own me. They may advise, but not control me. My life is my own. My conscience may not be regulated by count of noses, heavy bank accounts, or the nod of society. And the word of God is not bound. My tongue is my own, and I may not be forced to a position of prudent silence, when conscience and duty say speak. I may explode, too, in the presence of wickedness and no one in the land of the free and the home of the brave may deny me the right. I may speak and take the consequence. I may speak and die. But if I do not speak I surely die."

Reproof is becoming a lost art. We may compliment, but not reprove. Especially we may not rebuke influential sinners. This is not prudent. But when administered reproof is severe discipline. "Them that sin," says Paul, "rebuke before all, that others also may fear."

It has a cleansing effect. While some may quit church and cease supporting it, their influence is largely broken. Others will heed the voice of warning and straighten up their lives.

There are Scriptures that seem to justify proper exercise of discipline. Paul wrote to the Ephesians, "Have no fellowship with the unfruitful works of darkness, but rather reprove them." To the Corinthians: "I write to you in an epistle not to company with fornicators. Therefore put away from among yourselves that wicked person."

Jesus gives instructions on how to proceed when one has transgressed. "Moreover if thy brother shall trespass against thee, go and tell him his fault between thee and him alone; if he shall hear thee, thou hast gained thy brother. But if he will not hear thee, then take with thee one or two more, that in the mouth of two or three witnesses every word may be established. And if he shall neglect to hear them, tell it unto the church; but if he neglect to hear the church let him be unto thee as an heathen and a publican."

The steps of procedure with the offender are plain: "Tell him alone. Talk the difficulty over lovingly with him alone. If he will not hear thee, take one or two with thee." Discreet friends will increase the probability of settlement.

"If he shall neglect to hear them, tell it to the church." Tell it to the church as a last resort. Let the wisdom, love and prayers of the church be united to settle the trouble.

"But if he neglect to hear the church, let him be unto thee as an heathen man and a publican."

CHAPTER XLVII

WHY MEN DO NOT ATTEND CHURCH.

There is an alarming neglect of God's house so that the question is often asked why men do not attend its services more regularly. The following are suggested as some of the reasons:

1. They don't want to go. And with many, "don't want to," is an end of the argument.

2. They are tired and want rest. But worship is restful to both soul and body. The man who attends worship on Sunday is best fitted for Monday's work.

3. Others are not properly dressed. Pride, laziness, drunkenness or misfortune is the ailment in this case.

4. The church is not alive to its mission. The preacher may be dull, the members unsociable, or living in sin, sustained and courted by the church because of their money or social position.

5. The truth condemns them. Their lives are not right and conscience accuses them and their hearts are not at rest.

The clear presentation of the truth frets, angers or discourages them, and they avoid it like a sore eye veils itself from the light.

The singing, the prayer, the sermon, the open Bible, the very stillness and sacredness of the hour arouse conscience, so that its voice seems to say, "you are a sinner."

6. Worldliness is a fruitful source of non-church attendance.

The cares, business and pleasures of life fill hand and heart and brain, so that many have no time nor disposition for God's house. Reading secular papers, buying, selling or looking over the ledger; drinking, carousing or sleeping; visiting or receiving visitors occupy the hours of the sacred day. "God is not in all their thoughts."

Many make the holy day a holiday. They may be found by tens of thousands on the river, in the woods, on railway trains and street cars or buggy riding, in parks and on base-ball grounds. They bow at the altar of pleasure.

In a city in Indiana, on a certain Sunday, it is said, the Christian church had a congregation of seventy-one persons and the Presbyterians eighty-one. On the same day five thousand persons witnessed a base-ball game.

7. A lack of conscience makes against righteousness.

Men do not feel their responsibility. Conscience may not greatly trouble them for neglect or evil doing. They say "we feel all right, therefore we are all right."

Conscience is not a safe guide, if under the dominion of selfishness. It may be scarred and hardened by sin. A deadened conscience may no more respond to duty than a blind eye sees the light.

8. Men are unbelievers. They boast of "free thinking," look wise and say they have no use for church or Bible.

They not only stay away from church but make it unhandy for their wives to go. Many a professing Christian wife has told the writer that her husband was not a church member nor a believer which made it doubly hard for her to live right and go to church. How shall two walk together except they be agreed? Much infidelity is sheerest hypocrisy springing out of the fertile soil of egotism. A shabby cloak to hide sin, it is often renounced in the honest hour of death.

9. Many are not trained to attend church. Their parents did not take them by the hand and lead them to the house of God. Church going is a habit, and a good habit. If the children of this generation are trained to reverence God's house the men and women of the next generation will be reverent worshipers in His sanctuaries.

> "'Tis education forms the common mind,
> Just as the twig is bent the tree's inclined."

10. "There is no church of my denomination near enough for me to attend." Nonsense. Who are you that you can't worship and bow down before God anywhere with His people? If there is no church in your community start a cottage prayer meeting, organize a Sunday-school, have "the church in the house." Do something. Do it quickly and keep on doing it.

Most of the reasons for non-church going are makeshifts. They are but excuses. They will not stand the test of truth, nor the fires of the judgment day. Men will not present them with confidence in the honest hour of death. And God will sweep away "the refuge of lies."

May God arouse the slumbering consciences of men for "their feet go down to death, their steps take hold on hell."

CHAPTER XLVIII.

WHY MEN SHOULD REGULARLY ATTEND CHURCH SERVICE.

1. The church is God's house. It is called "the house of God." It belongs primarily to no man or body of men.

2. God commands it. "Not forsaking the assembly of yourselves together."—Heb. 10:22.

3. It is a "house of prayer."

4. Men live, and they need the inspiration to right living that comes from the Sanctuary.

5. "It is appointed unto men once to die. But after this the judgment."—(Heb. 9:27.) For these two epochs in their destiny, men need preparation. They have souls to save or lose forever.

6. Men have commanding influence. They set the pace for society. What the men are, society strongly inclines to be. Where men go to church their wives and children occupy places in the pews. Their boys will be in the Sunday-school.

7. The example of men attending church silently favors the church. They do that much, at least, to keep the church from dying out.

Many churches once alive and flourishing have closed doors and are a roosting place for owls and bats because the men neglected God's house and gave time, strength, money and love to other things.

8. The best and noblest men in the world's history have been reverent worshipers in God's house, and they

have owed much of their inspiration to the public teaching of God's Word.

9. Multitudes who have been converted, lived successful Christians, and are safely housed in Heaven, point to God's Holy House as their start and stay along the way of life.

10. A man can make no single investment that will pay a better dividend in his life and character and the well being of his family, than to be a faithful supporter of the public worship of Almighty God.

The community in which he lives and rears his family will be the gainer in intelligence and morality by his care of God's house.

"Finally, brethren, whatsoever things are true, whatsoever things are honest, whatsoever things are just, whatsoever things are pure, whatsoever things are lovely, whatsoever things are of good report, if there be any virtue, and if there be any praise think on these things.—Phil. 4:8.

CHAPTER XLIX.

PRAYER ANSWERED.

"But thou when thou prayest enter into thy closet and when thou hast shut the door, pray to thy Father, which is in secret, and thy Father which seeth in secret shall reward thee openly."—Matt. 6:6.

Precious truths are revealed in this scripture. How minute the instruction. The worshiper is to enter his closet and shut the door. He is assured that he is not alone. God is with him to behold, where no human eye can see, and openly reward the secret seeker.

An illustration impresses the writer that prayer is a power that

"Moves the hand that moves the world."

A new church had long been needed in the community and attempts had been made to build.

The minister and his wife presented the subject in its various phases before the Lord, taking no step without meditation and prayer.

The time seemed inauspicious. The failure of the wheat crop immediately affected the farming community. Leading members did not think the time ripe to undertake a project requiring general and united effort.

The minister and his wife, affected by the prevalent sentiment, were deterred for months from aggressive work. They were convinced then that a church was needed, and that the people were able to build.

They had stood for a pure church finance, against worldly methods of raising money, and had given largely of their income. They had presented a full gospel, stood for God and truth at the risk of reputation and believed that God would honor their faith in building for his glory.

They prayed for wisdom and courage, the hearts of the people and a revival of God's work.

Spending the day with one of his members, the building idea was broached and immediately opposed. They directed conversation into more congenial channels.

After dinner this member brought up the church project and, strange to say, favored building.

Calling for pencil and paper he commenced an estimate of amounts the members should pay to build a church that would "reflect credit upon the community."

Right heartily did they survey the field, consider the availability as well as the ability of men and women who composed that particular church and community.

Perhaps they did not think the work they were doing would materialize into more than "a church on paper." But in the light of events, the incidental meeting, uncalled and unofficial, was important, for God was in it, though they knew it not.

After the party dispersed, the minister, as if bent upon a mission called on another member who, though favorable to aggressive movements in the church, was hopeless of results in this case.

He, however, consented to visit with the pastor, a wealthy widow to enlist her aid. She consented to her assessment and was in sympathy with the movement. To the surprise of the community twelve hundred dollars were soon subscribed.

This member became an efficient helper in all the work of building.

Two thousand dollars conditionally subscribed impressed the official board. They said, "We have not before had such prospects, and we cannot ignore the subscription. These names represent our best people and their sentiment in a substantial way, upon this subject. Let us rise and build."

And "the people had a mind to work." To-day a neat, substantial structure, in a pretty, inland village, costing four thousand dollars is an accomplished fact.

Not that building churches is unusual, or that the structure is costly in an age of fine churches but "the secret of the Lord is with them that fear him and he will show them his covenant."—Psa. 25:14. The pastor and many spiritual people look upon the little church as a monument to answered prayer.

As he went about his work and saw one loading sand, another hauling brick, others mixing mortar digging the foundation and laying brick, heard the sound of hammer and saw, was with the officiary of the church planning ways and means, and observed the structure rising toward heaven, he said, "it is God's doings. He still hears and answers prayer."

Though prayer for the building of the church commenced in the pastor's home, the secret was communicated to spiritual people who pledged to keep the work and workers before the Lord. The prayer circle widened. The gifts were prayers and received as from the Lord. And all the work went on in the spirit of prayer and thanksgiving.

The scripture that heads this article stands out to the writer like raised letters of gold.

Prayer is a power that should be cultivated by God's children. It may be used in every mood and in all the range and sweep of life.

Laboring men, widows and orphans may employ it to secure employment and money. In sickness and trouble direction and help may be secured in a thousand ways.

Young people choosing companions may inquire of God and find help in every time of need.

"If any of you lack wisdom, let him ask of God that giveth to all men liberally, and upbraideth not; and it shall be given him. But let him ask in faith, nothing wavering. For he that wavereth is like a wave of the sea driven with the wind and tossed. For let not that man think that he shall receive anything of the Lord."

CHAPTER L.

WHY PRAYER IS NOT ANSWERED.

"I desire thy blessing, dear Lord; I am willing to be or do anything for thy glory; only grant me thy favor."

The prayer comes from a heart desirous of the "best of gifts."

God is waiting to be gracious, and seeks to answer prayer. Testings come. God tries the soul; the devil tempts; the world offers its bait, and the flesh seeks to seduce.

A worker in the Lord's vineyard is needed. Your fitness is urged. You excuse yourself, and, upon earnest solicitation, say, "I will not change my mind."

Another does the lowly work if that desert "shall rejoice and blossom as the rose."

Now the prayer. You desired "the best of gifts." The Lord heard, and would answer. He permitted trials, heart-searchings and the discipline involved in granting the petition. The whole nature must be fitted to a plane compatible with the special high gifts that we would enjoy. The life of faith, with its special temptations and trials, is the soil out of which springs the prayer of faith.

The answer to our prayers would so surprise and disappoint us that the Lord in infinite love tests us to see if we will have the petitions we desire.

Faith, obedience, love were tried. At each point an unyielding "No" was registered.

Was this not of the Lord? Does he want his children to do uncongenial things? Was there an element of uncertainty in the call? It came through man. The circumstances were untoward. The work required self-denial and promised no immediate reward.

The refusal was not uncertain, however urgent the call.

God speaks through his Spirit, Word, providence, friends, enemies; even the wicked may voice his call.

He says: "My child, I sought to promote you in my kingdom, but you would not. I put the knife to pride and you drew back; I strained to strengthen, but you cried, 'I'm weak, the burden is grievous to be borne!' I would polish, but you refused the friction; I would refine your gold, but you resisted the flames. You ask to be excused; I also excuse you from the blessing of peace and power, and the desire to be greatly used in extending my

BEST THINGS COST MUCH.

kingdom among men. Upon the whole, you do not desire the things you ask. They cost too much. I have trusted souls who are emptied of sin and self, cleansed and filled with my Spirit. They are a peculiar people, zealous of good works. Quiet and little among men, they are often unknown to the world, and unappreciated by it. They have counted the cost, and make themselves of no reputation. They are willing to sweep a street or rule an empire at my will and for my glory. These I fill with revelations of wisdom and love, and send on special missions of mercy. You will not pay the price. You are unwilling to humble yourself, that you might be exalted. You may take a lower place and do a lower work. Only 'take heed that the light which is in thee be not darkness."'

CHAPTER LI.

PRAYER AND POLITICS.

A preacher was approached by leading members of his congregation to secure his vote for their candidate.

His party had no candidate for Representative, and they thought that he might be willing to vote for their friend. The case was urgent, they argued, as the opposition was making a desperate effort to defeat a good man

The pastor felt the force of their appeals. Three considerations weighed upon his mind:

His party had no candidate for Representative. He could cast a full party ballot and vote for his friend.

The candidate was a temperance man. Do we owe nothing to friendship? If one would have friends he must show himself friendly. Besides, sober men are to be encouraged. And isn't temperance temperance, whether in one party or another? Why not be rational?

The office seeker's family, connected with the best people in the community, were members of the minister's congregation and supporters of the church. Is it nothing to be politic? May we not be right without unnecessarily alienating friends? Indeed, "the better part of valor is discretion."

The minister cordially heard their appeals. In fact the matter had been on his mind as a problem. He knew, as the election approached, that the delicate question must be settled.

He replied: "I appreciate the situation. A man's duty is not always clear, but I will give the subject careful thought, and will vote for Mr. ——— if I see that it is right."

To those who would understand, he said, "I am making my duty a subject of fasting and prayer."

One, in the heat of party zeal, warned the preacher that his interests were at stake; that he could not afford to be independent, but would need favors as well as other people.

The preacher replied, "I trust that personal considerations shall not unduly influence me. I will do right as I see the right."

He made his political duty a subject of fasting and prayer—considering it from every point of view. The Bible was freely consulted as the only rule and the sufficient rule of our faith and practice.

2 Cor. 6:14-18, weighed heavily upon his heart: "Wherefore come out from among them and be ye separate, saith the Lord, and touch no unclean thing and I will receive you; and will be a Father unto you, and ye shall be my sons and daughters, saith the Lord Almighty." The ten commandments, thundering, "thou shalt not," from Mount Sinai, have not been revoked.

The purpose of Christ's manifestation, to destroy the works of the devil, was considered.

The compromised condition of the church affected him.

The candidate, a pleasant gentleman, a temperance man, and a member of church, was headed for the Legislature—the law-making body of the state.

Committed to the license system, if elected his vote, voice and influence would license, not exterminate, the saloon. He would be permitted to regulate, if not too obnoxious to the liquor element, but never to strike a death blow to the rum power.

Of all candidates the position of Legislator is central, pivotal and influential.

He rose from prayer, Bible study, conversation, and a restudy of temperance and prohibition, in the light of the pleading candidate and his friends with an answer of peace, strong in the conviction that no reason existed for making him a specialty that would not favor the entire license policy. He saw that license is an approach to prohibition with no provision to secure it.

When argued that prohibition is impracticable, and does not prohibit, it ought in fairness, to be added that the ten commandments are violated every day but the Almighty does not revoke them.

The sermon on the mount is still the Christian's standard, even if after nineteen hundred years the church fails to stand squarely on Christ's platform.

One reason remained for voting for him, and that was personal. But personal interests were not sufficient to lay aside a principle.

The answer of peace assured him that he must stand for the prohibition of all evil, including the liquor curse, both in prayer and voting booth. And this he must do at any cost to his popularity, the risk of losing friends, salary and position.

He came out of the contest a more thorough Prohibitionist, better grounded in the faith, with the conviction that a faithful God hears and answers prayer.

His vote that day left no shadow upon the conscience of the man who regarded his political duty sacred as worship. He voted as he prayed and was at rest. "This is the victory that overcometh the world even your faith."

CHAPTER LII.

PERSECUTION.

Yea, and all that will live godly in Christ Jesus shall suffer persecution. II. Tim. 3:12.

The gladness of the Christian life, the peace afforded by the Gospel and the gain of personal piety are frequent themes of Christian pulpits. Not so many sermons are preached on the trials and persecutions of the righteous, and yet the afflictive element is manifest in every true life and abundantly set forth in the New Testament.

UNPALATABLE TRUTH.

This is unpalatable truth. It is not popular. Fear of offending the weak and discouraging the young, may cause ministers to postpone discussing the graver issues of Christian discipleship.

The result, however of not presenting the losses and crosses, as well as the joys of the Christian life, comprehensively, is that many commence the service of Christ with immature views and inadequate conceptions of its duties and responsibilities.

CAUSE OF FRUITLESS LIVES.

Hence the fruitlessness of many lives. They expect sunshine, singing birds and blooming flowers, but when clouds hang over their heads and thorns beset their path they grow faint-hearted and weary. They say: "We did not know this. We did not expect difficulty and danger. We thought that the Christian life was one long summer day; the path strewn with flowers, and birds making melody in the trees." Is not the Christian life one of peace and happiness? Will not the Lord raise me up friends? Will he not give prosperity? Why these reverses? Why opposition and neglect? Why is my path one of difficulty and danger?"

It is evident that many members of the church have never counted the cost of discipleship.

THE WORDS AND SPIRIT OF JESUS.

Let us keep close to the spirit and words of Jesus: "Whosoever doth not bear his cross, and come after me, cannot be my disciple. For which of you, intending to build a tower, sitteth not down first, and counteth the cost, whether he have sufficient to finish it? Lest haply, after he hath laid the foundation, and is not able to finish it, all that behold it begin to mock him, saying, "This man began to build, and was not able to finish.' Or what king, going to make war against another king, sitteth not down first, and consulteth whether he be able with ten thousand to meet him that cometh against him with twenty thousand? Or, else, while the other is yet a great way off, he sendeth an ambassage, and desireth conditions of peace. So likewise, whosoeth he be of you that forsaketh not all that he hath, he cannot be my disciple."

JESUS DID NOT FLATTER MEN.

Jesus did not flatter and cajole men into the kingdom. He did not say; "If I make plain the cost of discipleship men will turn from me." But to the multitudes he said,

"You follow me for the loaves and fishes. Consider well; are you able to be my disciples? Do you know what it involves? I make no promise of earthly gain or honor. Foxes have holes and birds of the air have nests but the Son of man hath not where to lay his head."

His course seemed impolitic, if he would win followers or set up his kingdom on earth.

POPULAR RELIGION.

There is a popular religion. It excites no opposition. It encourages pleasures of the world and conformity to its fashion in business, politics and social life. It opposes no sin specifically. It lacks aggressiveness. It does not stem the tide of worldliness but floats with the prevailing current.

The Scriptures are fulfilled in all man pleasing professors: "Woe unto you when all men shall speak well of you; for so did their fathers to the false prophets."

"How can ye believe which receive honor one of another, and seek not the honor that cometh from God only."

THE CHRISTIAN LIFE A WARFARE.

The Christian life is a warfare. Its conflicts are real. Satan is vigilant. There is spiritual wickedness in high places. Unreasonable and wicked men oppose themselves. This results in conflict; so that the Scriptures are ever true, in a world lying in the wicked one; "All that will live godly in Christ Jesus, shall suffer persecution."

There are those who apply this Scripture to the early church. And it may be so applied. In the first centuries of Christianity many sealed their faith with their blood. The apostles all suffered violent deaths except perhaps one. Martyrs of the cross are numbered by millions. But thanks be to God the blood of the martyrs is the seed of the church.

Others include heathen lands in the fulfillment of this Scripture. This is also true—Behold the boxer uprising in China and the opposition to the Gospel in every heathen land. The conflict that ensues where the Gospel opposes barbarism and every evil known to low civilization is a life and death struggle. The sword is unsheathed in every land where the Gospel is preached.

But hatred to the Gospel in heathen lands does not compass the full meaning of the apostle's words. The Holy Ghost says, "all," and we may not add to or subtract from the Word of God. Emphasize "all." Let the word have full force. It means every one.

Human nature is the same in every age, and clime. The spirit of the world has not changed since the days of Christ. It is the same in Christian and heathen lands. The devil is not dead, nor is he converted, though he may unite with the church. Christ's kingdom is opposed to Satan's kingdom.

The antagonism is real. Light opposes darkness. Sin is arrayed against holiness. The Gospel wars eternally with evil. Truth and error are at antipodes. It is the nature of things. This is eternally true.

The gospel is arrayed against ignorance, intemperance, slavery, lust and all iniquity whether in Czar or peasant; millionaire or beggar; bishop or layman; whether in America or Africa, in the first or twentieth century.

The Gospel is a message of peace on earth, good will toward men. It brings light, love and blessing to every heart and home and land. Life and salvation follow its glorious wake.

Where it has sway the desert blossoms as the rose, and the wilderness and solitary place are made glad.

And yet the Prince of peace is a man of war. He stands at the entrance of every heart and home and land with drawn sword, saying: "I come to send a sword." History proves it.

Spain for hundreds of years held Cuba in bonds of superstition, ignorance and cruelty. But the light of Christian civilization spreading over the earth, unsheathed the sword of justice and broke the bonds asunder.

A few years ago old China waked in violence only to yield great liberty to the Gospel's beneficent sway among its benighted millions.

Russia is attacked within and without by the sword. The spirit of the Christ in the hearts of men demands larger liberty, larger manhood and the rights that come to man as man. It is not autocracy but manhood that Jesus Christ would redeem. But this means the drawn sword, where arrogance and selfishness entrench themselves against the onward march of truth.

The Gospel unites everything that is true, pure, good and holy. It cements as adamant all that is lovely and of good report. The just and right are indissolubly one forever.

THE GOSPEL DIVIDES.

But the Gospel divides everything unholy and impure. It has no fellowship with the unfruitful works of darkness but rather reproves them. Injustice, lust and inhumanity are no part of the Gospel, however strongly intrenched in law and countenanced in high places. A count of noses does not settle the gospel's claim.

PARENTAL TIES BROKEN.

Parental ties have been broken in godless families by one child becoming a Christian. The peace and quiet of death may have reigned before, but war began when the humblest child became a Christian.

A member of the church, converted to Christ and to Protestantism said that his father tried,more than once, to kill him for being a Christian.

A young lady was opposed by her family after becoming a Christian. The spirit of persecution was carried so far as to affect her health, break down her nervous system, and commit her to an Insane Hospital. In her treatment and committal to the asylum her pastor and friends felt that injustice had been done a sanctified child of God. The Scripture was fulfilled in her experience: "A man's foes shall be they of his own household."

An evangelist, who accepted Christ when a boy, was at his father's command examined to see if he was insane on religion. The lawyer, who was a Christian, said: "The rest of us would do well if we had as sound minds and as good hearts as he." But he was disinherited and lost a patrimony of $10,000 for fidelity to Jesus.

But the evangelist said with a smile of victory, "The Scriptures are fulfilled in my life; in giving up father and mother, houses and lands, and my own life also, I have received a hundred fold, fathers and mothers, houses and lands, with persecution, and the promise of everlasting life."

"Jesus I my cross have taken,
All to leave and follow thee.
Naked, poor, despised, forsaken
Thou from hence my all shall be;
Perish every fond ambition.
All I've sought, or hoped or known."

This beautiful hymn is said to have been written by a child of wealthy parents, who had been driven from home and disinherited because of accepting Christ.

If this be its origin, what wealth of meaning is given to the sentiment:

"Let the world despise and leave me.
They have left my Savior too:
Human hearts and looks deceive me,
"Thou art not like them untrue.
And while thou shalt smile upon me,
God of wisdom, love and might,
Foes may hate and friends may shun me,
Show thy face and all is bright."

BLESSINGS WITH PERSECUTION.

Blessings are promised to the Christian, "a hundred fold, now in this time." Hear it ye fearful. I have found it true. But, one little proviso in the will connects all life's blessing "with persecution." This is the Christian's legacy. It is the will. And the will cannot be changed. It cannot be broken. The Christian will be blessed. The meek shall inherit the earth, but the inheritance involves persecution. "With persecution," is the reading of the will. Rejoice, rejoice, oh children of God.

REFINED PERSECUTIONS.

The follower of Christ may not be thrown into prison or burned at the stake. His property may not be confiscated. But he will be persecuted.

His afflictions may consist of slights and insults. His reputation may be attacked. Social ostracism may be his portion. He may suffer in the sensibilities and not in prison.

But "all that will live godly shall suffer persecution." It is not *may* suffer but *shall* suffer persecution.

HE WAS NEVER PERSECUTED.

Professors of religion without persecution for Jesus' sake, may question whether they are followers of the meek and lowly Jesus.

A Christian woman relating her experience in the sanctified life told of persecution. Her pastor, a genial gentleman, said that he had been a minister many years and had found the Christian life a pleasant one. He had many friends and no enemies that he knew. He had never been persecuted and knew nothing of that experience.

Another lady, bright and consecrated, who knew the character of this pastor's ministry said, "I could tell Brother Blank how he would suffer a little prosecution for Jesus' sake. Let him speak openly against the saloon; stand an avowed enemy of whiskey; denounce Sunday base ball, Sunday visiting and Sunday desecration generally. Let him fall upon his knees and seek till he finds the experience of entire sanctification and then stand on his feet like a man and witness definitely to the blessing and preach it. I think he will know something of persecution. He will suffer, if he is true."

Christian wives quietly suffer neglect and injury at the hands of husbands who hate Christ. Children taught by Sunday-school teachers are deterred in the Christian life by godless parents. Christian workmen in shop and factory amidst beer drinking, swearing, wicked companions endure rebuffs, jibes and scorn. Consecrated business men suffer ostracism for principles of righteousness. Godly employees lose positions because they will not work on Sunday and in other ways violate God's holy laws. Ministers of the gospel are sacrificed at the hands of worldly churches.

But time would fail to mention the protean forms that the spirit of evil assumes to afflict God's children. It is sufficient to know that "all that will live godly in Christ Jesus shall suffer persecution." Thank God for patience and holy courage that cheerfully endures all for Jesus' sake.

Jesus says: "If the world hate you, ye know that it hated me before it hated you. If ye were of the world, the world would love his own; but because ye are not of the world, but I have chosen you out of the world, therefore the world hateth you. Remember the word that I said unto you, The servant is not greater than his lord. If they have persecuted me, they will also persecute you; if they have kept my sayings, they will keep yours also. But all these things will they do unto you for my name's sake, because they know not him that sent me."

THE CHRISTIAN'S LEGACY.

"Marvel not, my brethren, if the world hate you." "The world knoweth us not because it knew him not."

With these Scriptures, the history of Christianity, and

the experience of every true child of God, let the disciple of Jesus —

EXPECT PERSECUTION.

Do not wonder that it comes. Wonder if it does not come. "Many shall be purified and made white and tried." First purity, then trial. It is God's order.

PURITY AND PERSECUTION ARE TWINS.

"For unto you it is given, in the behalf of Christ, not only to believe on him, but also to suffer for his sake." We talk much about believing, little about suffering. Believing is one part: suffering "for his sake" is the other. Both are God's plan.

Persecution should be "for righteousness sake." "Blessed are they which are persecuted for righteousness sake, for theirs is the kingdom of heaven." He who will live holy in an ungodly world will know what it is to suffer. Injustice hates justice. Dishonor despises honor. The thief dreads honest men. Impurity cannot endure purity. Sin cannot tolerate holiness.

Persecution should be for Christ's sake.

A professor of religion punished for an ugly spirit, a hasty temper, injustice or lust is no credit to the church.

A fanatical, self-willed member of church may suffer affliction' but he should not deceive himself by thinking that he is suffering for Christ's sake. He is suffering

FOR HIS OWN UNWORTHY SELF'S SAKE.

He may be getting his just deserts.

The evil that men speak of Christians should be false.

If accused of lying, drunkenness and fraud, the reports should be untrue.

It is not detracting from the truth, that Christians are afflicted on account of their goodness, to say that many suffer because of irregularities, eccentricities and fanaticism. Their lack of meekness, gentleness and love invites antagonism.

Self-willed, sharp-tongued, narrow and bigoted, they

RUN AGAINST THE NATURE OF THINGS

and cry "persecution."

They are getting their deserts. Their goodness and sense are receiving a severe test.

Many fiery spirits break at this point. It is easier to fly the track and become frenzied religionists than to be meek and lowly, and love and suffer like Jesus.

BEHAVE YOURSELF.

God's children should behave like Christians while in the furnace of affliction. Are you slandered, hated, evil entreated?

What shall you do? The message of Jesus is plain. "Love your enemies, bless them that curse you, do good to them that hate you, and pray for them which despitefully use you, and persecute you. That ye may be the children of your Father which is in Heaven."

Bless them which persecute you: bless and curse not." "Recompense to no man evil for evil." "Avenge not yourselves, but rather give place unto wrath." "If thine enemy hunger, feed him; if he thirst give him drink. Be not overcome of evil, but overcome evil with good."

NO EASY TIMES.

We should endure trials. Are you determined to avoid suffering for Christ's sake? Is it settled that you will be had in reputation with the ungodly? Is it your purpose to be popular with worldly sets and wicked men? Then you have within you the seeds of disloyalty to God. "The friendship of the world is enmity to God. Whosoever will be a friend of the world is the enemy of God. "Whosoever will save his life shall lose it; but whosoever will lose his life for my sake the same shall save it."

As professors of religion we demand easy times; pleasant sailing, no storms; many friends and no enemies.

But the Christian is a soldier. He is made for battle. He must be strong and brave to endure hardness as a good soldier.

PRAISE IN PERSECUTION.

The Christian should rejoice in persecution. Jesus enumerated indignities to which his children would be subjected and said: "Rejoice, and be exceeding glad; for great is your reward in Heaven; for so persecuted they the prophets which were before you." "Blessed are ye when men shall hate you, and shall separate you from their company, and shall reproach you, and cast out your name as evil, for the Son of Man's sake. Rejoice ye in that day, and leap for joy; for behold, your reward is great in Heaven, for in like manner did their fathers unto the prophets."

Christians are literally to

JUMP UP AND DOWN FOR JOY

when afflicted for fidelity to Jesus.

"The apostles, before the council for preaching Jesus,

rejoiced that they were counted worthy to suffer shame for his sake.

Persecution is a blessing in disguise. It is God's way of making holy character. It gives firmness to moral fiber and fineness of finish to character that no school of culture can impart.

Pampering Christians, feeding them rich viands, dressing them in silks and broadcloths, honoring them, makes fat and heavy, gross and sensual, pleasure-loving professors, but

PERSECUTION REFINES THEM,

makes stalwarts of men. The strongest and noblest specimens of manhood have passed through the fires of affliction.

Flesh and blood do not invite trials. But they come if we are true and they bring with them their own reward.

Persecution is

THE SECRET OF POWER.

Power is so costly that most Christians conclude, much as they desire it, that they cannot afford it. If the Christian would have power let him obtain purity of heart, witness, live and stand for it. Then will come persecution and with it power.

Stand true, child of God, in the furnace of severe trial and you will have the power you crave. The fire will burn the bands that fetter you. Nothing valuable will be lost in the flames. Out of every trial God will deliver and bring you forth

MORE THAN CONQUEROR.

Afflicted one, if your motives are pure and your aim single to the glory of God; if suffering for righteousness' sake, you are accused and condemned "falsely," rejoice, jump up and down for joy.

You are entering into your inheritance. You have this badge of discipleship, this mark of special favor: The world hates you and it hated your Lord: Rejoice and be exceedingly glad, for great is your reward in Heaven.

A PEEP INTO HEAVEN.

The curtain of Heaven parted a little and the Revelator was given a view of the redeemed. What did he see? Whom did he behold?

"A great multitude which no man could number, of all nations, and kindreds, and peoples, and tongues, stood before the throne, and before the Lamb clothed with white robes, and palms in their hands. And one of the elders answered, saying unto me, What are these which are arrayed in white robes? and whence came they? And I said unto him, Sir, thou knowest. And he said to me, These are they which

CAME OUT OF GREAT TRIBULATION,

and have washed their robes, and made them white in the blood of the Lamb. Therefore are they before the throne of God, and serve him day and night in his temple: and he that sitteth on the throne shall dwell among them. They shall hunger no more, neither thirst any more; neither shall the sun light on them, nor any heat. For the Lamb which is in the midst of the throne shall feed them, and shall lead them unto living fountains of waters: and God shall wipe away all tears from their eyes."

CHAPTER LIII.

GRIEVING THE HOLY SPIRIT.

The puny arm of man may be raised against the Holy Spirit of God, so that He may be grieved from the heart and cease to warn, convict, comfort or guide.

The question is how do we grieve the Holy Spirit. I propose to speak of ways not generally alluded to.

There is a tendency to relegate Christ to the church service, the Sabbath, and the ceremonies of religion.

We meet the monitions of the Spirit saying, "I am baptized, and belong to church, and partake of the Lord's supper. I support the institutions of religion."

God's spirit touches every department of life and works outside of the prayer-meeting, and on other days of the week besides Sunday.

We grieve the Holy Spirit by adopting public opinion as our standard of life rather than the Bible. There is a religion of public opinion," but it never saves the soul from sin.

UNWILLING TO BE A MARKED MAN.

Many aim to be nothing more than average Christians. They are satisfied and expect to conform to the world around them. A preacher on his death bed repented that he had striven to be only an average minister. He was unwilling to follow the Lord wholly—to be peculiar, to be a marked man for God. He would avoid the offense of the cross by following the well beaten path of ordinary Christian living.

Others are more concerned to be held in public favor than to be right. They will not give themselves to the work of rooting out sin. That would not be popular. "What would Jesus do?" is not their serious thought.

The Holy Spirit is grieved when we are governed by the spirit and ways of the world in business.

The Bible is the sufficient rule of faith and practice.

A man may say, "I know that the law of justice and benevolence should govern business. The course I pursue may not be right, but it is the way of the world. I have all sorts of competitors—Jews, infidels, and the wicked, who fear not God nor regard man. Their motto is success. I have a family to support and educate, and he who provides not for his own household is worse than an infidel. Besides we have the church to keep up. And while the things a business man resorts to may not be right, he is deserving of consideration for he has much to contend against."

I know a young man who was a member of church and clerk in a retail store. Reared in a country Christian home, his ideals of the Christian life were high. After going into the store he said to a relative, who was also a church member, "I do not believe it is right to charge two or three prices for the same article of goods. She replied, "I think that you are very particular and conscientious." "Well," he replied, "I can't help it; that's the way I feel."

He continued in the store for years, but ceased to be regular at Sunday-school, and was often too tired, or for other reasons, did not attend church. Religion is fast losing hold on him. He is likely never to be heard of as a power in the church of God.

I know his employer. In early religious life he was devoted to God. His conversion was marked. Fervent in spirit, he labored to bring sinners to Christ. But he has secured wealth. To be rich became his ambition. His instruction to his clerks is, "Never fail to make a sale." To-day he is without spiritual power in the church. His voice is never heard in prayer. Occasionally attending church, he is not regarded as liberal nor devoted but backslidden and worldly.

I am persuaded that thousands of business men, by resorting to what are regarded shrewd trades, which may be practical dishonesties, are Sampson-like shorn of strength. If they remain in the church they are formalists. Thousands of others have given up a profession of Christ, and church membership, as a burden too grievous to be borne.

We sometimes ask, "How can we reach business men, the brainy men of affairs?" It is a question of their yielding to honest conviction, and being willing to get right with God and man at any cost.

Business men are to do business for God, as preachers are to preach for His glory.

The Christian cannot be a worldling in politics. A man says of politics, "These are my civil duties," and of religion, "These are my Christian duties. The one is secular and belongs to the world; the other sacred and belongs to the church. Politics and religion can't mix. Politics must not interfere with religion, nor religion with politics. If religion invades the realm of politics it will get smirched, and if politics clasps hands with religion it is an unholy wedlock. Be wise and keep such opposites apart."

Religion is great, it includes all. If it does not control a man's business and politics, and his whole life, in every relationship, it is because he has it not. It means everything in the world to be a disciple of Jesus. He must be first.

A VOTE AND PRAYER.

I would not dictate men's political views and actions, but one cannot be politically wrong and religiously right. If a man's heart is wrong in politics, he is not right toward God.

A Christian must vote right as well as pray right. What is a vote but a prayer—an expression of opinion, desire, will? So is prayer upon bended knee. The one must not conflict with the other. If the prayer at the ballot box contradicts the prayer at church or in the closet, God will answer the ballot-box prayer, for he has put his heart and life into this one. He only "said his prayers" in the closet and at the church altar.

The Christian must stand before God with his politics and say, "Oh, Lord all is surrendered to Thee, my politics, my party, and the candidates. I will vote and do all for thy glory." He may feel ignorant and needy, but, he will say, if he is to stand clear before God and his conscience, "My heart is open to Thee. Pour in the light and I will follow Thee, wholly and forever, and know no other master."

A CHRISTIAN IS NO MAN'S TOOL.

The professor of religion cannot be a thing, a tool, a mere machine in politics and a man of God anywhere.

What must be said of the practice of buying and selling votes? It is a violation of law and a menace to our institutions. He who buys votes and he who sells his vote are outlaws and should be deprived of the right of franchise. They are traitors, not patriots. They are enemies of our government.

What do sinners think when professors of religion adopt and uphold measures which they know to be corrupt? They see us determined to beat the enemy, by fair means if possible, but bent upon success. If the wicked see professors of religion fall in with their tactics, right or wrong, they judge that there is nothing in religion—at least in these professors of religion. They are a stumbling block in the way of sinners. They misrepresent Christ and are dead weights in the church. They act like sinners and are sinners. They are selfish, inspired by the love of the world, the flesh and the devil.

The professor of religion who follows the fashions of the world grieves the Holy Spirit. Uniting with the church we declare that we renounce the world, the flesh and the devil; turn our backs upon the world; repent of pride, ambition and self seeking, saying, we will not be governed by these things or live for them. We promise to follow the meek and lowly Jesus in the way of humiliation and the cross. How opposed to this is the spirit of conformity to the world, manifested in display, and show, and style in dress, furniture, houses and in every way which the natural heart can devise.

By patterning after its fashions, professing Christians do not convince the world that they are living for God and eternity.

Permitting the mind to dwell much upon fine dress, elegant furniture, beautiful houses and surroundings involves the mind and heart in dissatisfaction. Changing these with the changing fashions necessitates expense of money, time and strength which might be used for the gospel. This type of professor is prevalent in the church. But he lacks the single eye to God's glory and much of his life's work must be wood, hay and stubble.

CHAPTER LIV.

USE OF HOLINESS.

Holiness is central in the Bible. It is the subject of promise, command, exhortation and prayer. The sacred page fairly glistens with it in doctrine, biography and song. Patriarchs, prophets and apostles wrestle "with the angel" for the blessing, and in its might subdue sin, work righteousness, obtain the promise.

The Methodist Church born in a holiness revival, considers this doctrine central in its scheme, and itself raised up to "spread scriptural holiness over these lands."

What use is the doctrine and experience of entire sanctification in this busy world in practically working out the problem of human life?

1. Live it. The devil says, "Live it," with a hiss. The world says, "Live it," with a laugh. The church says, "Live it," as the only hope of my redemption and the recovery of a lost world to Christ. Finally, the Lord says, "Live it," with the promise of certain victory.

Holiness is not a luxury, but a necessity. It is not cake for the few, but the bread of life for the millions who spend their "money for that which is not bread, and their labor for that which satisfieth not."

The mother needs holiness to keep her patient with children tagging at her heels, her hands full of labors, and her heart engaged with cares.

The business man needs it to keep him true and sweet amidst the strife of trade.

The laborer, with a family to support, educate, keep in society and church, with wages small and uncertain, needs its life to keep him from sinking into discouragement when engaged in a seemingly losing contest.

Live holiness in a world of sin and sorrow, and holiness will live in you a power to keep you pure, courageous, loving, and more than "conqueror through him that loved you."

2. Labor in the strength of it. It is a pleasure to eat, but this is not the sole end of eating. Food must be transmuted into nourishment of brain and muscle, and these into strength for thought and action.

Holiness is food and it is strength. There is work to be done, battles to be fought, Jerichos of sin to be taken, Philistines to be routed. These require strength, and the spirit of sacrifice. Holiness is to this end. It prepares its possessor to do hard work easily, and make sacrifices without loss from friction, produced by fretfulness or "injured dignity," but with rejoicing that it is counted worthy to suffer for Christ.

Holiness is the solution of the mission problem, both as to men and money, and of the liquor question. The labor agitation can be permanently settled on the basis of the golden rule, which is impossible without the pure, humble love of God and man filling the heart.

3. Be a witness of it. A blessing, strength, joy in your life, let others know its power. Advertise it. "Ye shall be witnesses unto me." "Out of the abundance of the heart the mouth speaketh"—not ought to speak, but speaketh. Men's tongues tell on them. A dumb holiness is dead. Holiness not confessed by life and lip is already vanquished. "Live it, but don't confess it?" Confession is part of the life—the tongue's part in the life—of ho-

liness. And the tongue plays an important factor either in holy or unholy life.

4. Preach it. Every Christian is a witness. Paul was both minister and witness. Every preacher is to be a witness and a herald. Proclaim the glad news that Jesus came into the world to "save the people from their sins;" that the blood of Jesus Christ cleanseth "from all unrighteousness."

This is God's truth. His word is full of it. He is responsible for the truth. He did not consult us as to what the message should be, but says, "Preach the Word."

Will men despise the message and forsake the messenger? We are not commanded to be successful, but faithful. Is the one impossible? The other is imperative. But the sure word of promise is, "My word shall not return unto me void, but it shall accomplish that which I please, and it shall prosper in the thing whereto I sent it."

The Church is suffering defeat because of a mutilated, adulterated gospel.

THE FEAR OF MAN IS A SNARE.

Fear and unbelief add to or take from God's Word. Hear the fearful warning: "Be not afraid of them that kill the body and after that have no more that they can do. But fear him which after he hath killed hath power to cast into hell: yea, I say unto you, fear him." A wholesome fear of hell would bring multitudes of professors whether in the pulpit or pew to their knees crying for pardon and holiness, and then to their feet with glad hearts and wide-open mouths declaring what God has done for their souls.

God's word to every one who would speak in his name is: "See that thou make it after the pattern shown thee in the mount.

CHAPTER LV.

GIDEON'S BAND.

Seven years Israel had suffered under the Midianites. Driven to dens and fastnesses of the mountains they sowed crops, only to see the enemy burn or trample them down by their droves of camels.

Their heart-broken cries were heard and God forgave their sins.

An obscure and humble instrument was chosen to deliver Israel. The trumpet call of the prophet gathered the people to the defense of their nation. Gideon was confronted by the strange announcement, "the people are too many." "What, thirty-two thousand 'too many' to meet an army of one hundred and thirty-five thousand? Is it possible that I am mistaken? Am I laboring under a delusion? Is it indeed the divine voice that I hear?"

Though the army is to be reduced, God respects the choice of men. The prophet proclaims, "Whosoever is fearful and afraid let him return and depart from Mount Gilead." The proclamation in modern phrase would read: "Let all cowards quit the camp at once." Twenty-two thousand men stepped out of rank. These represent many halting church members. Willing to be saved, they would be soldiers and have "a little hand" in the victory—if sure of victory. But when a stand means possible defeat or death, they conclude it unwise to take the risks. "There is no use fighting against terrible odds. A man may throw his life away. And what's the use of that? A living dog is better than a dead lion.' '

Are they not supported by public opinion? The respectable following, more than two to one, is a good showing for any cause. Men of wealth, women of social position, honorable senators, wise doctors, able lawyers and judges of law and popular preachers recognize the right, but say it is unwise to go forward. "For fools rush in where angels fear to tread."

"I CAN'T" DOES NOTHING.

The cowardly multitude retards the work of God. Their understanding would make foolish the wisdom of the Almighty. Hear their concerted wail: "We can't pray. We can't witness for Christ. We can't sacrifice money or time. We can't support missions or go as missionaries. We don't believe in holiness. No man can live without sin. We can't conquer the foe. We shall be slain, every one of us. We can't wipe out the saloon. We can't"—but why go on? The large word in their vocabulary is "can't." And they never do exploits for God because of unbelief.

Majorities do not avail. Plausible excuses are a refuge of lies. God says to the half-hearted, "stand aside, slink away to your hiding places. You will defeat the army." If Israel succeeds you will vaunt yourselves and say, "Our might and power have gotten the victory."

Ten thousand remain. "Too many" is again the fiat of the Almighty. Does God mean to mock his chosen leader in the presence of the enemy and all Israel? The second trial takes the men to the brook. All who lap water as a dog are selected to fight the forlorn hope.

THE BACKBONELESS.

Strange test. A little thing? But trifles reveal character. Whether something natural revealed the soldier, or a supernatural touch set aside God's own, we know not. But three hundred passed the examination. Three hundred satisfied divine inspection.

The first test eliminated the back-boneless. The second rid the army of those who lacked self-control, the spirit of self-sacrifice, the instinct of the soldier.

THE CRAZE FOR NUMBERS.

Nine thousand seven hundred were rejected. Nine out of ten were "too many" to fight God's battle.

Is this an object lesson thrown upon the walls of time, teaching that the craze for numbers side-tracks the church? Is it the hand-writing of God, saying, "I seek quality rather than quantity."

The epicure may decry strong drink, but he need look no higher than his stomach to locate his deity. Esau, whose belly was his god, has descendants like the stars of the heavens for multitude. A glutton may be respectable; drunkards are branded. But epicures are not God's soldiers.

PREACHERS EAT TOO MUCH AND EXERCISE TOO LITTLE.

Popular preachers have passed the dead line or into their graves at forty who might have been effective at seventy if they had put the knife to their throats when seated at sumptuous tables. Smiling hosts saying: "Doctor, take another piece of the cake, it won't hurt you. I made it with my own hands," are a temptation and a snare. If instead of saying, "Thank you, sister, just a little piece to taste," the popular pastor had been hero enough to say, "No, thank you, I prefer not to dig my grave with my teeth," he might have been in his pulpit instead of in his grave.

SLOTH AN ENEMY TO POWER.

The Christian will hear, if he listens, a still, small voice registering the amount he should eat.

Another suffers from sloth. He snoozes late in the morning losing hours that should be devoted to the Bible and prayer. But he loves the pillow. He prays, "Lord, lead and I will follow," but wonders that he does not increase power. Some string holds him. He does not swing free. The spirit is willing, passively willing, but the flesh dominates the spirit.

A GOOD, WEAK PERSON.

He is not outbreaking, but a good, weak person. Difficult work he cannot do. A lackey may do little things. Had he chosen to be king, God would have made him more than conquerer, mighty to pull down the strongholds of Satan.

Duty may lead to separation from wife and children for a season. The evangelist and missionary are strangers at home and at home among strangers. Because of the sacrifice of social ties he may say, "I cannot."

Business, social standing, ecclesiastical position, even life, must be subject to the call of God. One may respond, "I do not care but for those I love. I cannot see those dearer than life exposed to loss."

A LOWER GRADE MAN.

Like the red sea before the Hebrews stand the words of Christ, "If any man come to me and hate not (love not with a lesser love) his father, and mother, and wife, and children, and brethren, and sisters, yea, and his own life also, he cannot be my disciple." "He is not worthy of me."

Who wonders that he should be tempted to shield those he loves? But if a lower affection stands between the soul and Christ, a supreme allegiance has been denied. And the man really chooses an inferior place. He chooses to be a lower-grade man.

Innocent pleasures and the refinement of wealth are not condemned. Men enjoy comforts and luxuries which money, position or taste permit. And they say, "Are these not ours? Have we not a right to enjoy our own to the full? But they forget the higher right, appreciated by noble natures, to sacrifice lesser for greater good, to yield our rights for others' good.

When men choose easy, comfortable life, neglecting the higher calls of duty, they elect to stand among the large majority of common place people who express willingness to fight God's battles, but are not the men whom God can use.

CHAPTER LVI.

THE DEVIL'S SIDE TRACK.

A young lady who was a comparative stranger in the city to which her parents had moved, and who was desirous of meeting the best people of the church and comumnity, was honored with an invitation to spend the evening with friends in a prominent Methodist home.

She soon learned that popular games were the order. Invited to join in a game of cards she replied that she could not, as she had never learned. In the pleasantest mood they offered to instruct her. She reluctantly told them that she really did not wish to learn, as her parents had forbidden her playing cards, it being a violation of the rules of the discipline of the church, and they did not think it right for Christians to play cards or dance.

"LOST HALF HIS LIFE."

They treated her conscientious scruples as "really funny," assuring her that there was no harm in the games, or they would not engage in them. They were certain that by her scruples she had narrowed her life and missed a great deal of pleasure. It was jocularly said that one who did not indulge these innocent pleasures "had lost at least half of his life.' '

One other young lady said: "My grandmother plays cards and sent her children to dancing school. She thinks that these amusements are all right and she's a good Christian. And I am a Methodist, and play cards and dance too."

ALMOST ENSNARED.

"Well," said the young Christian, "I did not indulge the games, though in a Methodist home and a number of good people of the church spent the evening that way. But, I confess that I thought the whole question of amusements over as I had not done before. And I came to the conclusion, surrounded by the pleasant, social atmosphere, that dancing and card-playing are only wrong to those who had promised the church that they would not indulge in such amusements.

"Fortunately our revival began and I joined the voluntary choir, became enthused in the meeting and got better acquainted with good church people and am a better girl than I was before the meeting, though I had not entered into temptation."

"The sermon on Popular Amusement by the evangelist impressed me. Christians are a separated people. I had not thought of it so before. I had always tried to be on good terms with all church members, good, bad and indifferent. But I see it differently. It is settled. I will find my associates among devoted Christians and will not try to harmonize the Bible, the church and Christian living to please worldly professors."

ALMOST RUINED BY PROFESSORS.

And she is a consecrated, Christian girl, cheerful and helpful to her mother at home, to her father in the office and to pastor in church work.

Pleasure-loving professors have a proper place in her thought and heart, but they will not be permitted to weaken her faith or influence her life. But what a narrow escape she ran of being ruined as a Christian by prominent church members!

CHAPTER LVII.

THE KINGDOM FIRST.

(Matt. 6:33.)

God asks the first of every heart and life. The first of his love, time, money and talents belong to God. No man can change God's order without hurt to himself and the kingdom.

Bible Christians are "a peculiar people, zealous of good works."—Titus 2:14; Separate from the world.—2 Cor. 6:14-18; Rom. 12:1, 2.

Shoals of infidels are made by church members who deliberately withhold part of the price, serve God with a divided heart, and relegate the Lord Jesus to a second place when he will have the first place.

It will make a world of difference which is first:

Self or God.

Money or the kingdom.

The world or Christ.

Pleasure or duty.

The lodge or the church.

Business or religion.

Housekeeping or the House of God.

Politics or religion.

Feasting or fasting.

Worldly conversation or Christian testimony.

Sin or righteousness.

Socials or revivals.

The lecture or preaching.

The play house or the house of God.
Happiness or holiness.
The novel or the Bible.
The concert or worship.
Gossip or secret prayer.
The newspaper or the Word.
The theater or the prayer meeting.
Sunday visiting or Sunday observance.
Policy or principle.

Reader, your choice, deliberately made, will result in character and destiny, will build or permit to go into decay the house of God. God search every heart.

CHAPTER LVIII.

A LOVE LESSON.

The house needed repairs of various kinds, but the landlord, miserly, exacting and unjust, had refused to make them. The renter, a Christian man, was seeking to be wholly the Lord's. He would do nothing un-Christian. In this particular case he would suffer inconvenience and loss rather than be unjust or even unkind. Improvements being necessary, he decided again to see his landlord. But, before going, he prayed for patience and a right spirit, regarding these more important than his rights. In the interview he requested that the property be put in better condition.

"I told you," said the landlord, "that I would make no further repairs on that house."

"But they are needed," said the renter. "I ask what is reasonable. It is a matter of business. The rent is high. You are careful to collect it in advance, and you ought to keep the property in good condition. But I can't compel you. There is one thing I can do. I can move."

The last sentence touched the landlord's heart or pocketbook. Dropping his head, he said, after a moment's reflection, "What did you say needed doing on the house?"

The renter, in a frank and kind manner, named the different items, and without waiting for reply, bade him good evening. He walked away in the light of the setting sun, meditating upon the situation, particularly the attitude of his heart toward the man whom he had gradually come to consider a thorn in his flesh. He queried with

MAN'S EXTREMITY IS GOD'S OPPORTUNITY.

himself, "How did I conduct myself toward Smith? Was I patient? Did I have a right spirit?" He thought, "Well, I controled myself; I did not get angry." And he could not condemn himself for want of patience.

But he questioned, "Why can't I love Smith?" He knew that he did not. He was conscious that every effort revealed a dead heart toward him. He knew that love is the essence of religion. The true Christian loves every man, whatever his character. He must love the disagreeable and unlovely; the snarled and crooked, the unjust, unkind and cruel. "I say unto you, love your enemies, bless them that curse you, do good to them that hate you, and pray for them which despitefully use you and persecute you." He had honestly tried. While he did not hate, he could not love him. And he knew not what to do. Almost in despair, he looked up and said, "O Lord, I do not love Smith. I cannot. I have tried and failed. But I would give the world if I could. Help me." He meant every word, and would have given any amount of money or the last thing he had on earth to love the man whom he knew to be mean and unlovable.

MAY LOVE BUT NOT LIKE.

He had reached the end of his strength, but his extremity was God's opportunity. Immediately he felt that his "heart turned over," and he loved the man whom he could in no wise like. He had the victory. His heart was satisfied, and greatly rejoiced. He saw the faults of the selfish man as plainly as ever, and deplored them. But he had learned a lesson of love which he will not soon forget. He does not depend upon his emotions. Love may exist as a principle without emotion. He regards the attitude of the will. When this is right, whatever the state of his feelings, he unhesitatingly declares, "Yes, I love. I love my enemies. I love all."

CHAPTER LIX.

A RIGHT SPIRIT.

"Ye know not what manner of spirit ye are of." Luke 9:55.

A VINDICTIVE SPIRIT.

The disciples, John and James, preceded Jesus on his way to Jerusalem. The inhabitants of Samaria did not receive Jesus because his face was turned toward the metropolis. This angered the disciples. They inquired, "Lord, wilt thou that we command fire to come down from heaven and consume them even as Elisha did?" But he rebuked them, saying, "Ye know not what manner of spirit ye are of."

A long-standing prejudice existed between Jews and Samaritans. The disciples thought that they were influenced by a proper zeal against the enemies of Christ and their nation.

The church has had too much such zeal. Persecution of Christians has sprung out of this spirit. The fires of hell have kindled at this altar.

A NARROW, BIGOTED SPIRIT.

John upon another occasion manifested the same spirit. They forbade one casting out devils in Jesus' name, because he followed not with them. Jesus said, "Forbid him not: for he that is not against us is for us."

Christian toleration is the lesson. John would have

every one follow his company. They must utter his shibboleth or be misunderstood, disbelieved and come under ban.

That he cast out devils did not count; that he did it in the name of Jesus did not satisfy. He did not follow with them and so was not right. John rebuked him, but Jesus rebuked John for narrowness and bigotry.

MUST BELIEVE OUR CREED.

Many fail to see good in any who differ from them. They must follow with us, train in our company, belong to our church, party or school, believe our creed, utter our watchword and submit to our tests, or be suspicioned and cast out as evil-doers.

There are church people who are strained to see good in members of other denominations. They can't think others are right because they don't think as they do and follow with them in every particular.

It is so in politics. People look over high walls of party prejudice with distrust into the ranks of other political parties, and are in danger of regarding neighbors and friends as strangers and enemies.

PERSONAL AMBITION.

In the midst of Jesus' mighty miracles reasonings arose among the disciples as to which of them should be greatest.

Thoughts of self rather than of Christ and others occupied their minds. His mighty works were seen and his marvelous words heard with strife and envy rankling in their bosoms. Which shall be greatest? Which have the chief seat? Who shall rule? Who have the pre-eminence? How unworthy, but how natural.

One may be possessed of these dispositions and scarcely know the motive that animates him. He may have a wrong temper and not know it. He may think others wrong and himself right. He may imagine that he has proper zeal, is contending for truth or fighting the good fight of faith, while his inspiration may come from ignoble passions.

If a man builds a house it is something tangible: he sees it, lives in it, and walks around it. But his spirit is himself, and he is busy looking without. His spirit is looking, feeling, hearing. Interested in himself, he is prejudiced in his own favor. It is difficult to see himself as he is.

He explains or excuses his sins and shortcomings. He often looks upon his brother with critical eye, judges him, sees the worst in him, exaggerates the evil and minifies the good.

We need to pray, "Create within me a new heart and renew a right spirit within me."

"A new heart" and then "a right spirit"—continually "a right spirit."

CHAPTER LX.

LIGHTS IN THE WORLD.

On a corner opposite the parsonage, in a village, a gas light shines night and day. Its rays are seen a long distance.

To-day the lamp is lighted as much as it was last night, but it is not seen any more than the post upon which it stands. Even an electric light does not add luster to the sun.

I have thought that the lamp shining day and night might complain and say, "I am alone on the top of a post. Through long watches of the night, in wind and cold and heat and rain, pestered by insects I shine. All would be darkness, but for me. But no one cares for me."

But the lamp was made for darkness. The sun eclipses its light.

We may be holy amidst moral darkness. The Christion in the family or workshop may complain that he is alone, that his life is uninfluential and attended with difficulties. But he might remember that darkness adds brilliancy to the light. Night is the light's opportunity.

People may not consult the honor of the lamp, or see it, but they see by it. They seek safety or convenience. Light is necessary. The traveler sees the path and avoids stumbling, pitfalls and winding ways.

The Christian is not an original light, but reflects the brightness of the Son of God. Conspicuous as a candle upon a candle-stick or as we would say, an electric light upon an arch, he "cannot be hid."

"Let your light so shine." You cannot make it shine,

but let it shine. Permit it to be seen. Remove hindrances and give opportunity.

The adverb "so" is a hinge that turns a thought. It directs the manner of shining. The Christian is to "so shine."

His good works glorify God. Self, seen as such, hinders the light. Christ is to be lifted up.

The Christian's blameless life reflects the power of Christ to save in the midst of a crooked and perverse nation among which he shines as a light in the world.

Attempts to hide our light is neither a proper conception of Christ nor our mission.

We are not to pray on the street corners to be seen of men, nor let our left hand know the almsgiving of our right for self-glorification. This direction discounts Phariseeism. But Christians are the light of the world. As such they are to shine brightly and openly before men.

"His lamps are we,
 To shine where He shall say,
And lamps are not for sunny rooms
 Nor for the light of day.
But for dark places of the earth,
Where shame and wrong and crime have birth;
Or for the musky twilight gray,
Where wandering sheep have gone astray;
Or where the light of faith grows dim,
And souls are groping after Him;
And as sometimes a flame we find,
 Clear shining through the night
So bright, we do not see the lamp,
 But only see the light,
So may we shine—His light the flame—
That men may glorify His name!"

CHAPTER LXI.

LIVING BUT DEAD.

An evening party was given in honor of the school teachers of the township. After an elegant supper the young people engaged in conversation and innocent games. These were well planned and elicited thought and interest.

When the tide of enjoyment was highest, an observer said the ladies look most beautiful, and the men most noble. Interested and full of energy they were at their best.

Of one it was said, "She is full of life—the life of the company. I like life, not death. I have no use for dead people."

In the church we need life too, the life of God. God cannot use dead people. Many members alive to the world are dead to God.

An undertaker was conducting a funeral in the absence of the pastor. Wishing to make suitable remarks upon the life of the deceased he said: "This corpse was a member of this church for many years." The ludicrous blunder suggests a comparison: There are many spiritual corpses who are members, in good and regular standing, of all the churches.

We have seen the galvanic battery applied to the limbs of a dead frog causing it to perform strange freaks as though possessed of life. But when the battery was removed the quiet of death reigned and the work of decay went on undisturbed.

We have seen church members under external pressure, as a revival, go through certain motions as though there was life within which caused activity. But when the pressure was removed the evidence of life was gone also. They bore no fruit. They gave no sign of being born of God. Men may turn the church into a social club and a kind of interest, activity and life may abound without the regenerating grace of God, and the life giving spirit. The life may not be spiritual. It may be social, literary, or political life. The unspiritual may be deceived but God is not mocked.

The church is often manned by dead men—dead spiritually, dead in trespasses and in sins. A dead man in the pulpit; dead men in the pews; dead men on official boards. The Sunday-school is manned by a dead superintendent, and the children are taught by dead teachers. How sad the sight or the very thought. Lord, breathe upon these dead that they may live.

"Spirit of life, and light, and love,
Thy heavenly influence give;
Quicken our souls, our guilt remove,
That we in Christ may live."

CHAPTER LXII.

JESUS TEACHING FAITH.

"According to your faith be it unto you."—Matt. 9:29.

The difference between heathen religions and the religion of the Bible is that the former is a system of works, by which the worshiper seeks to merit salvation; the latter is one of simple faith in Jesus our Savior.

The natural heart desires to substitute works for faith. It pleases the flesh, ministers to pride. God says: "by grace are ye saved through faith; and that not of yourselves: it is the gift of God; not of works, lest any man should boast."

Jesus was a great teacher of faith. When he opened blind eyes, healed the sick, cleansed the leper, or raised the dead, faith was usually the human condition of the miracle.

The church in all ages has given a double significance to Christ's miracles, seeing the fact and the spiritual teaching.

"And behold, there came a leper and worshipped him, saying, Lord, if thou wilt, thou canst make me clean. And Jesus put forth his hand and touched him, saying, I will: be thou clean. And immediately his leprosy was cleansed" Matthew 8:2, 3.

INSTANT SALVATION.

Leprosy is a type of sin. It is incurable. This leper worshipped Christ, had faith in him, and was immediately cleansed.

So the sinner seeking pardon or the believer purity, by faith in the ability and willingness of Christ to save, is instantly pardoned or purified.

"But Jesus turned him about, and when he saw her, he said, 'Daughter, be of good comfort: thy faith hath made thee whole.' And the woman was made whole from that hour." Matthew 9:22.

This woman had been diseased twelve years, suffered many things of many physicians, spent all of her money and was nothing better, but rather grew worse. One touch of faith made her whole.

The sinner's disease of sin may be of many years' standing and very aggravated, but one touch of the heart of Jesus by faith brings the healing balm.

"And when Jesus departed thence, two blind men followed him, crying and saying, Thou son of David, have mercy on us. And when he was come into the house, the blind men came unto him, and Jesus said unto them, Believe ye that I am able to do this? They said unto him, Yea, Lord. Then touched he their eyes, saying, According to your faith be it unto you."

Jesus directly appeals to their faith in his ability to restore them to sight. When that was complete, he touched their eyes, and they were opened.

Soul-sight is restored in answer to faith in a mighty Savior. " Believe ye that I am able to do this?" is the question Christ asks of every seeking soul.

"And Jesus said unto him, If thou canst believe, all things are possible to him that believeth. And straightway the father of the child cried out, and saith with tears, Lord, I believe: help thou my unbelief." (Mark 9:23, 24).

The son had a dumb spirit from a child, which caused him to foam at the mouth, gnash his teeth, pine away, fall on the ground or into the water or fire. The disciples had tried, but failed to cast him out. How pitiable the condition! "But if thou canst do anything, have compassion on us and help us," is his wailing cry to Jesus.

Jesus made the son's healing a question of the father's faith: "If thou canst believe, all things are possible to him that believeth." Then, evidently out of a desperate struggle, the father said with tears, "Lord, I believe, help thou mine unbelief."

Sometimes the soul, struggling against an inveterate habit of doubting, must "desperately believe" against all odds and seemings.

ONLY BELIEVE.

"Therefore I say unto you, what things soever ye desire, when ye pray believe that ye receive them ("have received," R. V.), and ye shall have them" Mark 11:24.

Pardon, cleansing, keeping power, come in this category. We are taught to believe that we receive them, now receive them, as we ask for them. As we pray we are to believe, and as we believe we receive.

I pray as a convicted sinner, "Lord, pardon my sins." I am to believe as I pray that he hears me. As a believer I pray, "Lord, sanctify me wholly." I am to believe that it is his will, even my sanctification. I am to receive it as a gift; receive it as I am; receive it now by faith, and I shall have it as my experience. Wonderful promise! A mighty stimulus to faith.

WE ARE DOUBTERS NOT BELIEVERS.

"O fools and slow of heart, to believe all that the

prophets have spoken!" (Luke 24:25.) Jesus could address his children in the same language to-day. We deny, criticise, philosophize, explain away, darken counsel by words without knowledge, do almost anything but believe. We are called believers, but as one has said, we might almost as truly be called unbelievers.

O brethren, let us get to our work of believing God without cavil. "Be not fearful, but believing."

"As many as received him, to them gave he power to become the sons of God, even to them that believe on his name" (John 1:12).

BELIEVING IS CENTRAL.

"For God so loved the world that he gave his only begotten Son, that whosoever believeth in him should not perish, but have everlasting life. He that believeth on him is not condemned, but he that believeth not is condemned already, because he hath not believed in the name of the only begotten Son of God. He that believeth not the Son shall not see life; but the wrath of God abideth on him." In three short verses the words believeth, and believe are found six times. Surely believing is central in Christ's teaching.

HEAD BELIEF AND HEART TRUST.

A difference exists between intellectual belief and heart trust. Two persons are standing at the end of a plank spannning a dangerous chasm, their only way of passage home. One says, "I believe the plank will bear my weight and carry me safely over, but I would not risk it for the world."

SAVING FAITH.

The other says: "I believe the plank is strong and a safe and sure way, while the only passage over the chasm. And I am willing to risk my life on it." He ventures on it, ventures fully, with whatever of caution or fear, and is safely delivered. When our belief in Jesus carries our hopes, prospects, present, future, soul, body, life and all with it, we exercise saving faith or faith that saves.

Faith may be effectually hindered. "How can ye believe which receive honor one of another, and seek not the honor which cometh from God only?" (John 5:44.) "Only believe, only believe" may not be the advice a seeking soul needs. There are states of heart in which to believe is impossible. When there is a spirit of self-seeking, when we will have reputation among men, the eye of the soul is not single. Spiritual vision is clouded. The fallow ground must be broken up. Thorough repentance, including confession and renunciation of all sins, inward and outward is needed. Self-dependence and slavish love and fear of man must be renounced. The soul from its depths must be able to cry,

"Thou, Oh Christ, art all I want!"

Then it will be able to exclaim,

"More than all in thee I find."

CHAPTER LXIII.

TO PROFESSORS OF HOLINESS.

"Stand fast therefore in the liberty wherewith Christ hath made us free."—Gal. 5:1.

Free in Christ, stand fast in this liberty. Having made the start, continue the life of holiness. He that continueth to the end shall be saved. There is more in living a wholly sanctified life than in commencing it.

I desire to address some advices, as they have come to me in reading, observation and experience, to those who have accepted Christ in his sanctifying grace.

FAITH NOT EMOTION.

1. Learn to stand by faith. We are sanctified by faith, we live by faith, we stand by faith. Not by inward illumination or consciousness, but by simple trust in Jesus are we kept by power divine. It may be simple faith, stripped of all comfortable emotions, but it will be honored of Jesus. The soul wants feelings to lean upon, but feelings are not our Savior. Jesus will not divide his honor with another. Let faith by constant exercise become the habit of the soul.

CONFESSION OF HOLINESS.

2. "A state of holiness should be clearly and definitely confessed." "With the heart man believeth unto righteousness, and with the mouth confession is made unto salvation."—Rom. 10:10. A faith which we are unwilling to confess is not full faith. The heart and the mouth are

connected in salvation. This is God's plan. A silent holiness is a dead holiness. A worldly church will say, "Live holiness, don't profess it." But if Christ is denied in our silence we soon have nothing to live. Many of those who fall from this grace do so from failure to fully and clearly confess the work done in them. The testimony must be continuous as the life is continuous. Instead of the testimony to full salvation promoting pride, it crucifies the flesh and promotes humility. The necessity for Christian testimony is laid deep in human nature. The passions of love, anger, fear or jealousy as they are freely confessed with the mouth are deepened in the experience.

A beautiful variety of language is found in the word of God by which to define this grace. Entire sanctification, holiness, perfect love, etc. Often this grace is described without being directly named. We are not to avoid using God's own terms. He has named this grace, and to constantly substitute human language for the language of the Holy Ghost dishonors Christ, grieves the Holy Spirit, and dwarfs the soul.

TIMES FOR PRAYER.

3. Have stated seasons for prayer. At such times call the heart to account. See that the consecration is as clear and definite each moment as it was the first time you yielded all to Christ.

INTELLIGENT HOLINESS.

4. We must read. Ignorance, prejudice, superstition and fanaticism are not to the glory of God. They are not handmaids of true piety. God does not ask a blind faith but an intelligent one, founded on the word of God.

First of all read the Bible. It is God's book. In it God speaks to us. It is his letter to his children.

Read holiness books and periodicals. These are the most spiritual publications. They are coming from the press in cheap form to catch the eye of busy men and women. Many families take two or three secular papers, but cannot afford a religious paper. With hours devoted to current literature and but an occasional glance at the Bible and other spiritual reading, is it a wonder that there is much spiritual leanness and a large per cent. of backsliding after great religious awakenings? Read a well edited holiness weekly paper. It will be a constant incitement to holy living, and keep you informed in the aggressive movements of the church for the salvation of the world.

STAND TRUE IN A COLD CHURCH.

5. Be in the use of all the means of grace. Private prayer, Bible reading, family prayer, the social meetings and public preaching, are all necessary to the sanctified believer. If the church is in a cold state, and holiness is not understood or received, the more need of your attendance and testimony to full salvation given in an humble, loving, loyal spirit to the honor of Jesus. Besides, you need to keep in touch with men.

TEMPTATION NOT SIN.

6. The holy soul will be tempted, but temptation is not sin. Jesus was tempted in all points like as we are, yet without sin. A solicitation to evil resisted till overcome is not sin, and will not bring the soul under condem-

nation. Yielding to temptation is sin. Resist the devil and he will flee from you. Keep off his ground. While the devil tempts all men, some men tempt the devil. They visit the saloon, the unholy resort, associate with the worldly and wicked, do doubtful, sinful things, and then complain that they were tempted. Oh, no. They are mistaken; they tempt the devil.

LOVE IS OF GOD.

7. Love is "the greatest thing in the world." It is the highest gift of God. Love is God. God is love. Visions, illuminations, inward lights, revelations, signs and wonders are nothing compared with the pure, humble love of God and man filling the soul. He who loves most is most Christlike. Whatever gifts we have, however great our zeal for the cause, if we have not the pure, humble love of God, it will profit us nothing. We are none of his. We should avoid a narrow, bigoted, prejudiced spirit. A judging, censorious spirit is opposed to the word of God. A morose, fault-finding spirit is anti-holiness. "Sour godliness" is the corpse of holiness. A bitter, sarcastic holiness is a dead carcass, a stench in the nostrils of every living thing.

PRIDE IN DRESS.

8. As to dress: "We may not sit in judgment and apply a dress standard to test others who profess salvation. After general principles of humility and modesty, we must leave much to the judgment and taste of individual believers filled with the spirit and seeking to please Jesus in all things." Our discipline says, "Let all our people be ex-

horted to conform to the spirit of the apostolic precept, not to adorn themselves with gold, or pearls, or costly array." —1 Tim. 2:9.

GOLD, PEARL OR COSTLY ARRAY.

A Free Methodist minister who was wearing as good a suit of clothes as any gentleman needs, said that good clothes were cheaper and better than poor ones. How shall one know positively whether it is absolutely right to wear a ten or a thirty dollar suit of clothes? A coffee sack, open at both ends and thrown over the head, would take the place of shirt, vest, coat, collar and necktie. Or one might wear untanned leather and save more money for the poor and the missionary cause; but he would be on his way to barbarism, and soon be in need of missionary, civilizing and Christianizing influences. On the other hand, "gold, pearl, or costly array" minister to pride, and are a misappropriation of the Lord's money. Luxuriant, self-indulgent professors are a shame to Christianity, whose founder had his Gethsemane and Calvary.

HELP THE PASTOR.

9. Holy people are strong Christians. They will not cause their pastors unnecessary trouble or criticise them unkindly if they do not in all things fill their ideal. They will not expect pastors always to preach so-called holiness sermons. They have the varied interests of the church to look after. Patient with the pastor's short-comings, they will be his most self-sacrificing helpers, doing all in the name of the Lord Jesus.

WEIGHTS ARE WINGS.

10. Expect contradiction and opposition, losses and crosses of various kinds. Mr. Wesley says, these are principal means of growth in grace. They should be received as a part of the Christian's heritage. "In the world ye shall find tribulation. They that will live godly shall suffer persecution." This applies to the true follower of Christ to-day as well as to the early church. There is no escape. Do not complain of these things. Do not speak of them, especially in public meetings.

> "Go bury thy sorrow, the world hath its share;
> Go bury it deeply, go hide it with care.
> Go think of it calmly, when curtained by night;
> Go tell it to Jesus, and all will be right."

CHAPTER LXIV.

PREJUDICE.

During the days of slavery and the Civil War, the States south of the Mason and Dixon line generally prayed and fought for the institution of slavery, while those north banded against the iniquity. Would the division have followed a geographical line had the people been governed by equity and right?

Who knows how largely political parties, schools of philosophy and even churches have had their origin and support in the wish, which is said to be father of the thought, of leaders to have their way and recognition? Perhaps Methodism in the United States would be united were it not for the invisible something we call prejudice.

Who that has heard campaign orators, and reads the party press, but recognizes that facts are managed in the interest of "our party." And if facts do not suit "our party" the worse for the facts.

A divorce involving the principal families divided the church of which they were members, along family lines. Both sides contained good people—the best people, in some respects, of the community. They thought that they were reasonable, but something besides reason swayed their judgments for the split to follow the blood line.

BUT "CRANKS" TURN THINGS.

A merchant who had a large tobacco trade was an inveterate user of the weed. The lady evangelist who held meetings in the church of which he was an official among other evils arraigned the tobacco habit as opposed to science, Scripture and common decency. Nor did she hold merchants innocent, who sought to enrich themselves at the expense of men's degraded appetites.

This "professor" heard sledge hammer blows against tobacco, night after night. How did he meet the truth? To be just to him it must be said that he did not attempt to meet, but adjourned meeting the issue by saying to the evangelist with a loud laugh, "Oh, you are a crank." And boasted among his kind, "I told her she was a crank, that's all," and he laughed with men who hung their heads and laughed, too.

This was the argument of one who proposed to lead his church and the community.

THE ORGAN AND THE VIOLIN IN CHURCH.

A woman opposed the organ in church, but favored shouting. She told of a woman who did not believe in "excitement" in worship, but welcomed musical instruments and quoted "the Psalms to prove the divine right of the organ, but did not see the Scriptures which exhort people to make a joyful noise unto the Lord."

The attentive listener might reflect, "You are both one sided and unwilling to know the whole truth."

Another who could tolerate the organ drew the line at the violin. He said, "I can't bear the fiddle in the house of God. It is always used in saloons." The lady to whom he complained said, "According to that you ought never to sing or speak in church, for your voice used to be heard in oaths and bad language, while you were drinking in saloons."

Prejudice blinds the eye so that one cannot see things he does not want to see. Oh, he sees, "But—but—and, well—but—."

Prejudice is a form of blindness of which we say, "None are so blind as those who will not see." Light hurts the eyes, and to be rid of the light it closes them, or hies away into the dark, saying: "I don't see. There is no light."

PREJUDICE CANNOT BE ANSWERED.

Prejudice is a species of deafness of which it is true, "None are so deaf as those who will not hear." It is the man with fingers in his ears shouting, "I don't hear a word you say," and strange to say he may not be telling an untruth. He may be truthful, but to be so he must keep his fingers in his ears.

This quality of *soul* is not answered. Its argument is "as I said," and its index finger is pointed. Unwilling to know, it will not examine a subject. "I said it and I will stick to it," is final, and he "will not be convinced, though he be convinced."

PREJUDICE WALKS IN RUTS.

This spirit makes no progress. It opposes aggressive movements in church or State. It stays in the same ruts from year to year, and loves them, because they are ruts, and because they are old, and because they are his ruts.

How subtly this disposition works. One thinks he is unbiased, weighing equally all sides of a question, but the child of secret likes, proceeds along lines of his predictions. Starting with the inclination the reason for his choice become stronger and clearer. Generously admitting that truth may be on both sides, that on his is strong as proof of holy writ. Like a lost traveler moving in a circle he always fetches up at the same place.

Prejudiced against a person you cannot—will not—properly estimate his qualities. His virtues will be minified; his defects magnified. Favorably inclined you hide a multitude of sins and discover his excellencies. Certain it is that one has not reckoned with all the influences that sway a man until he has taken account of his wishes and hidden aptitudes.

A LITTLE, MEAN MAN.

Under its sway the malign passions thrive, the generous impulses starve. Love dwarfs; anger and hate fatten. Envy and jealousy grow like weeds. Gentleness, tenderness, purity dwindle like plants springing from the crevices of rocks. Peace is uncertain and shallow; unrest is the normal state of the soul.

Many a man free of the crimes of murder or arson, who would not steal, is bound hand and foot by a disposition that makes him a little, mean, contemptible man. He reminds one of a fish floundering in water, tied to a stake. The string and the stake say, "Thus far shalt thou go and no farther."

It remains to be said that there are innocent prejudices. All are under the influence of predilections, good or bad, innocent or harmful. A large part of our usefulness and happiness consists in placing ourselves under influences that tend in the direction of righteousness and true holiness.

CHAPTER LXV.

JUDGE NOT.

The language of our Savior does not teach that we may not think. We may estimate and know men. This is neccessary. We are told that we may know the tree by its fruit; that we may not cast pearls before swine and that we should judge righteous judgment.

A man's success and happiness depend upon a proper estimate of men. He must know men as a carpenter knows lumber; a grocer knows groceries; a stockman knows the markets and cattle, and an educator knows schools and books.

What is meant by judging? What judgment is forbidden? We may not be suspicious of men or think of them in a manner contrary to love. We are not to be censorious, nor given to evil thinking or speaking.

WE MAY NOT JUDGE.

God forbids it. He commands us not to judge. His word is "Judge not." And the Apostle asks, "who art thou that judgest another man's servant? To his own master he standeth or falleth."

We may not know. We may be mistaken. Everything that we know may favor our judgment, but we may not have all the evidence.

LOVE OF FINE THINGS.

The writer was acquainted with an excellent lady who seemed to love inordinately fine houses elegantly furnished, costly clothes, splendid equipage and the recognition of leading society people. Her friends felt that she was inclined to worldliness. And yet she seemed devoted. A Christian worker, she loved the church and was withal a sincere woman.

When she came to die, looking into the face of a friend who had thought that her mind was too much fixed on worldly things, she said, calmly and sweetly, "It is all right."

Her friend felt a gentle tinge of reproof, which lingers with him, though years have passed. He has since been a little chary of hasty criticism.

A member of church who was ordinarily faithful in attendance upon the services was absent one evening from prayer-meeting. Her pastor wondered and even questioned her absence. But what was his surprise to learn that upon that very evening she was suffering a great deal of trouble. Her son had run away from home; the father was searching for him; the house was in uproar and great sorrow was in the home. All this occurred at the moment that she was being misunderstood and viewed in a prejudiced light.

AN OLD SOLDIER.

In a small town an old soldier leaned upon his cane and tottering as a drunken man, walking the streets. He was spoken of as an excellent citizen and a good member of church.

A stranger thought "is that the stamp of manhood, the standard of excellence in the community? Is one who cannot walk erect on the streets a first-class citizen and a good church member?" But the spirit of criticism changed to sympathy when he learned that the gentleman suffered from a form of paralysis which unsteadied his nerves so that he reeled to and fro as a drunken man.

LIKE FOR LIKE.

"With what judgment ye judge ye shall be judged, and with what measure ye mete it shall be measured to you again." The critical spirit reacts upon you. The law of retaliation is in force here. It is like for like. He who judges harshly is judged harshly. Make no allowance for the frailties and faults of others and they will measure to you the same in kind. They will misunderstand, criticise and censure you. "You shall receive judgment without mercy who have showed no mercy."

PARTIAL VIEWS

A minister, in his family, was discussing leading church people of wealth. He did not think they gave adequately to poor, unfortunate humanity. The pastor said, that intelligent Christian people who read secular and church papers, lead church and reform movements, would certainly know of suffering and the need of money for charitable and religious purposes.

But the preacher's son said: "There is one thing to remember; you are a preacher, you read religious papers and books on aggressive Christianity. Your attention is called to the needs of the poor and afflicted, the work of the gospel, and the forward movements of the church, as their minds are not and cannot be. You study these questions. They study others. They employ men and are intent on making money, as you are bent on making your church go. Besides they may think that they do their duty in the employment of men. And you never employ labor. They give considerable money as compared with other church people in the community. You should not censure them but make liberal allowance for different environments."

THE GOLDEN RULE.

We do not wish to be judged. We shrink from being viewed in a prejudiced light. To rest under suspicion is not pleasant; to be thought of without charity is as cheering as to attempt to warm your feet upon a cake of ice. Surely the golden rule applies here: "All things whatsoever ye would that men should do to you do ye even so to them."

LOVE THE GREATEST THING.

The writer knew a sick man, who was dropsical and a great sufferer. He called upon him when in distress of mind and body, facing death. After prayer the sick man was baptized, professed conversion and united with the church. He seemed sincere and hearty in his new found faith. But afterward he would get angry, criticise the Almighty for his afflictions, even curse, speak harshly to his neighbors and then in sorrow and contrition would repent.

People asked the pastor what he thought about the convert's profession of faith, "Is it real? Is he truly converted?"

PUT YOURSELF IN HIS PLACE.

The pastor said, "one thing is clear, we must have charity. His suffering; the wasting away of his body; his blood turning to water; his brain poorly nourished, and the habits of a life-time asserting themselves in his extreme weakness and agony, all call for gentle thoughts, kind words and 'sweet reasonableness.' "

Put yourself in his place. Would keen criticism, or gentle thoughts, kindly deeds, loving words, more coincide with sickness that must soon end in death? Can we not defer severe judgment, even under the guise of a just sentence?

He has one Judge, who is too wise to err and too good to do wrong—we can safely trust him in His hands. For shall not the Judge of all the earth do right? Besides we are told not to judge for we are brethren and our office is not to condemn, but to save."

A SELFISH SOUL.

If we knew the struggles of men with their defects and the many attempts they make to attain victory over evil we would often sympathize rather than condemn even in the unsuccessful battles of life. A great heart said:

> "What's done we partly may compute,
> But know not what's resisted."

A school man, proud and cultured was in many respects the soul of honor. But an exacting, narrow, selfish nature was his besetting sin. If a man owed him he pressed him hard for the last penny. He wanted all and on time, making little allowance for poor and weak men in the struggle of life. He was strong, why should not others be strong?

He would lecture and scold his children. His excellent wife endured a good share of criticism, often at inopportune times. Seldom making mistakes—unless the judging spirit mars the whole of an otherwise excellent life—he is slow to excuse short comings in others.

A DREAM MAY REVEAL CHARACTER.

A friend, who was brought into intimate relations with him, dreamed that she entered his library without knocking. To her surprise she found him upon his knees in prayer. His engagement was so deep that he did not notice her. His words came slowly forth. There seemed a minute between each. In agony of soul the sweat stood on his brow.

Sorry to disturb him, she inwardly rejoiced that the defects in his character which were a trial to others troubled him deeply. The place was sacred as a "holy of holies." God was there. Venturing to approach she shook him by the hand and said, "God bless you," and left the room.

It was only a dream, "but since that time," she said, "I have sympathy for Mr. ———, he has so many other excellent traits of character." And he has.

ONE TOUCH OF HUMAN NATURE.

The writer had an experience that tended to soften his heart. One touch of his body brought the thought of sickness, sorrow and death vividly to his mind. As he lay upon his bed he was brought into sympathy with poor, aged, sick, unfortunate, erring men of which he keenly felt that he was part with faults and weakness and disease on his way to old age and—the grave—It was "one touch of nature that makes the whole world kin." As he thought and wept, in the darkness of the night, he wished that he could relieve sorry, distressed, dying men; that he could enlighten the ignorant, lift up the fallen, and with kind words and deeds relieve human woe, whatever might be the cause of it. There was no criticism, but sorrow and love for suffering, erring, unfortunate men.

He understood better the words spoken of the Savior: "He had compassion on the multitude, when he saw that they were as sheep without a shepherd."

Oh for deeper sympathy for suffering men, for the touch of gentleness that will heal not hurt, bless not curse sick, sorrowing, sinning men, needing sympathy and Christ.

CHAPTER LXVI.

DANGER SIGNALS.

Passing through the country, one will see devices to frighten pestiferous birds from chicken coops and gardens. Old clothes upon cross sticks with arms extended, bright tin cans or glass bottles swinging in the breezes reflecting the light, seem instinct with life. A dead crow on a pole is a fright to all intruders.

I am reminded that the holiness ranks have professors who do not represent real holiness, but wearing the garb frighten people from the doctrine and experience by their spirit and eccentricities.

DRESS.

The first danger signal I mention is dress.

The Scriptures teach plainness of dress. The Holy Spirit also writes the same truth upon truly awakened hearts. But few sanctified people adorn themselves "with gold, or pearls, or costly array." These are not in accord with a meek and quiet spirit, which in the sight of the Lord is of great price.

But when one harps upon dress, picks at people's clothes, makes trouble with merchants in selecting a hat or coat, or always feels called upon to testify that he is dead to fashion, he becomes a source of fear and dread.

Some boast of being delivered from pride who need to be saved also from "all filthiness of the flesh." Cleanliness is akin to godliness.

THE GOSPEL OF SOAP AND WATER.

Congregations composed largely of the poor, unchurched classes hear much denunciation of the fashions of the day. They need also to hear the gospel of soap and water.

GOD LOVES BEAUTY.

A young lady who gave herself to Christ at a meeting where plainness of dress was stressed became severely plain in her taste or prejudice. Her Christian mother would dress her suitably to her years, and the Lord had made her beautiful in form and feature; but she refused any trimmings, however simple, to relieve the monotony of her attire.

The reaction came. To-day she is without assurance, questioning everything, backslidden in heart, because of a mistaken notion of what is central in Christian living. Her eyes, taken from Christ, were directed to her own and other people's clothes. But salvation is not by dress.

MANNERISMS.

Others render themselves ridiculous by sanctimonious tones and mannerisms. They grunt, groan, pray, and testify like a funeral procession or a threshing machine running at full speed

RELIGION AND SENSE GO WELL TOGETHER.

They are cheap imitators. Know one of "the elect" and you know all. They use the same phraseology. If one says "glory" all say "glory." If one shouts all shout. If one claps his hands all clap hands. They go through certain exercises or imagine they are without "the power." If their sensibilities revolt against the grotesque performance they think they are influenced by the fear of man or the love of praise, and are worldly.

Sensible people conclude that if religion requires this they are not ready to be "peculiar people"—that is to be strange and queer and odd.

A CRITICAL SPIRIT.

Another "danger signal" is a critical spirit. The "I am better than thou" spirit constitutes itself censor of everything and everybody. Such spirit is destructive. When it finds way into the heart of a holiness professor he is as one standing with drawn sword, saying to all comers and goers, "You dare not enter the temple of holiness."

Holiness gives clear views of sin. Therefore perfect love is needed to cover a "multitude of sins." Where there is much light without a corresponding degree of love the professor, instead of attracting men to Christ, "repels" them from the cross.

It is dangerous to dwell upon other people's faults, except in a spirit of pity and love. We should look at people as we view their pictures upon the wall, at an angle and at a distance to get the best light upon them. Saying the sharp word instead of the kind one, whipping instead of feeding the sheep, driving instead of leading the lambs, indulging what is doubtfully called "righteous-indignation," our spirits become harsh, our tones loud, and our tempers severe .

When such people control society takes on the nature

of a court of trial. Everyone's character is judged. And nearly everyone is found wanting. The Church is going wrong. Love, genuine love, for men and faith in God is the cure.

EASIER TO BE SEVERE THAN GENTLE.

The critical spirit grows on what it feeds. The preacher having the icy spirit, preaching on hell, causes his congregation to feel that he would push sinners into the place of torment. It is easier to be severe than to be tender.

STONES AND CLUBS DON'T DRAW.

And there are pulpits that throw stones. Sheep go where they are fed. Empty racks or those filled with clubs and swords do not attract the hungry flock.

BUZZARDS AND THE CARCASS.

He who dwells upon evil cultivates a disposition to see evil. And he will feel impelled to denounce it. Thus increasing the power of denunciation, he comes at last to feel that he is not doing effective work unless striking at something or somebody. This unlovely state of mind grows abnormally. Proportionately with energy of spirit and conscientiousness will be the danger to himself, the church, and society.

Standing on a hill by a humble home, in the country as the sun was setting, I saw half a dozen buzzards alight on a large tree. I said to my friend, "A dead animal may be near that tree." He replied, "One of my large hogs died and I buried him there. I would not be surprised if they dig him up." It appeared that those fellows gathered in the evening to guard their treasure and get an early start on the morrow at their savory meal.

There are carrion-loving birds. And "wheresoever the carcass is, there will the eagles be gathered together." Scavengers are necessary. They cleanse the earth by filtrating its filth through their own bodies. But who would not rather be a lark than a buzzard; a nightingale than a carrion eater?"

HUMAN BUZZARDS.

And there are human buzzards, who see the evil in people and feed upon it. It seems right that they should—given to what they fondly call "righteous indignation." They wonder at other people's indifference, and call it sinful compromise.

They do not stress the tender love of God, nor enjoy hearing other people emphasize it. Such preaching seems lacking in loyalty to the truth. Besides, it must be admitted that it brings their harsh, flinty spirits under condemnation.

And yet "love is of God," and "God is love," and "love is the fulfilling of the law," and "he that loveth is born of God," and "love believeth all things, endureth all things, hopeth all things, and never faileth."

CHAPTER LXVII.

CHRISTIAN TESTIMONY.

A young gentleman was invited by a lady interested in his salvation to attend one of the services of her Church. It was a young people's social meeting, and the leader urged all to witness for Jesus .

One young gentleman arose, and told what a prominent minister said, and took his seat. Another related what a certain church did.

A young lawyer explained the nature of testimony. Heresay evidence, he said, would be ruled out of any court. The witness must know.

Others took the witness stand and spoke as much to the point.

RELIGION WITH A TONGUE TO IT.

At length, an old gentleman gave his experience of the love of God. He told of deep and pungent conviction and a clear and happy conversion. Afterward he found the Savior in a deeper work of grace, and now has constant victory, kept by the power of God.

Certain young ladies snickered at the old gentleman's story, and whispered loudly enough to be heard by the stranger, who was a careful listener, "The old man always gives the same talk."

The leader now asked the visitor to speak. He refused, giving as a reason that he was not a Christian. Being urged, he replied: "I am not a professor of religion; but since you insist upon all speaking, I will say, you called for testimonies for Jesus; and while several have spoken, but one has truly witnessed. The first speaker told what a minister said, the next what a certain church did, but neither bore testimony. The lawyer explained the nature of evidence, but failed to witness. The old gentleman gave a personal testimony of the love of God. He told of sins pardoned and a mighty Savior who gives him victory over every temptation and difficulty. He alone has witnessed for Jesus.

After the severe rebuke, the stranger took his seat, and the meeting was dismissed.

Much passes in social meetings for Christian testimony which is not of the nature of confessing Christ. In a low state of spirituality, almost any kind of sentimental talk will pass for Christian experience.

A Quaker, who was a leader of his meeting, never opened his mouth in praises of Jesus. He once said in a revival-meeting, under pressure, "When I have anything to

DO NOT JUDGE.

say, I say it; and when I don't have anything to say, I say it too." A girl, in a class-meeting, gave this as a testimony, "When I came here I thought I would not say anything, but now I have, and I am glad of it."

If such is testimony for Christ, we must make the most of it.

A man may preach, and not witness for Christ. He may exhort and grow eloquent on some theme connected with salvation, or complain of the sins of the Church and the wickedness of the community, and dodge the issue of a personal testimony of salvation from sin.

One may speak with the tongues of men and of angels, have the gift of prophecy, understand all mysteries and knowledge; but without the love of God shed abroad in his heart by the Holy Ghost given unto us, he can not be a witness for Jesus.

The child of God may lack culture or position; he may speak with a slow, stammering tongue; but his simple experience of the love of God, uttered in the power of the Spirit, backed by a godly life, will cause men to marvel and seek the Lord. A Pentecostal, witnessing Church will move the world.

"Ye shall receive power, after that the Holy Ghost is come upon you; and ye shall be witnesses unto Me, both in Jerusalem and unto the uttermost part of the earth."

CHAPTER LXVIII.

THE TONGUE.

"Death and life are in the power of the tongue."

A glance through the Concordance at the words speech, tongue, words and mouth, and then into the life, will convince one that the tongue is potent for good or evil. What is said of the tongue is predicated of the heart back of it, for out of the heart are the issues of life. The tongue being the organ it freely uses to disclose its true character .

"If any man offend not in word, the same is a perfect man, and able to bridle also the whole body."

The government of the tongue is made the gauge of completeness of character. The varied passions find more constant and ready expression through it than through any other organ of the body. How difficult of control. But in its government how sweeping the victory—perfection and the whole body, including all the powers of the soul, brought under subjection.

"The tongue can no man tame; it is an unruly evil full of deadly poison." Jas. 3:8.

God alone can tame the tongue and take the poison of asps out of it. A tamed tiger is a tiger still, and liable at an unguarded moment to spring upon its keeper.

The work of culture may be carried to a high degree in the unrenewed nature, but a new heart and a right spirit alone insure the tongue to be governed by the law of kindness.

TOO MUCH TALK.

"Whoso keepeth his mouth and his tongue keepeth his soul from troubles." Prov. 21:23.

"True! true!" is Dr. Whedon's emphatic comment on these words.

We seldom regret talking too little. It is easy to say too much even on proper subjects, with the general intention of doing right. We can talk ourselves out oif our religion. Deeply spiritual people are not great talkers. How often we trouble our souls by failing to guard the door of our lips!

"But I say unto you, That every idle word that men shall speak, they shall give account thereof in the day of judgment. For by thy words thou shalt be justified, and by thy words thou shalt be condemned."—Matt. 12:36, 37.

FOOLISH TALK AND JESTING.

We recognize God's condemnation of profanity, obscenity or blasphemy, but Jesus says for "every idle word we shall give account." The Holy Spirit writes the same truth upon every truly awakened heart. He gently condemns the soul for idle, useless or mischievous words. How searching! We cannot afford to trifle; too much is at stake. Our words are a true index of the heart. By them we shall be acquitted or condemned before the Judge of all the earth.

THE WHISPERER AND SCANDAL MONGER.

"Behold how great a matter a little fire kindleth. And the tongue is a fire, a world of iniquity; so is the tongue among our members, that it defileth the whole body, and setteth on fire the course of nature; and it is set on fire of hell." Jas. 3:5, 6.

A fire! Vivid description of an evil tongue. "Behold how great a matter a little fire kindleth." A match may occasion the destruction of a city, a forest or a prairie. Reputations have been blasted, needless suspicions created, neighbors, families, and Churches divided, and States involved in wars by evil tongues "set on fire of hell." The whispered slander, the profane oath, the false report, the obscenity of the unclean or the blasphemy of the ungodly! What a world of iniquity!

Our duty in a matter so important in every relation in life is fortunately not involved in doubt, but plain instructions abound in the Scriptures.

"Wherefore putting away lying, speak every man truth with his neighbor: for we are members one of another." Eph. 4:25.

"Let no corrupt communication proceed out of your mouth, but that which is good to the use of edifying, that it may minister grace to the hearer."—Eph. 4:29.

"Neither filthiness, nor foolish talking, nor jesting, which are not convenient; but rather giving of thanks." Eph. 5:4.

"Let your speech be with grace, seasoned with salt, that ye may know how ye ought to answer every man." Col. 4:6.

"But speaking the truth in love."

THE TONGUE AND THE HEART.

May we accurately judge the state of our hearts by our conversation? We often speak of the Jews of the Old Testament Scriptures as mere formalists, without "heartfelt religion." The prophet speaking of his people said: "Then they that feared the Lord spake often one to another: and the Lord hearkened, and heard it, and a book of remembrance was written before him for them that feared the Lord and that thought upon his name." Mal. 3:16.

Paul says of true disciples: "Our conversation is in heaven." Phil. 3:20.

And Jesus utters a universal truth; "Out of the abundance of the heart the mouth speaketh." Matt. 12:34.

If our conversation is constantly of business, pleasure, society or politics, it is an index finger that points unerringly to our treasure, and where the treasure is the heart will be also. What is the theme of conversation around the table and fireside? As professors of religion what is the most frequent subject of our conversation in the parlor? The gossip of the day, or the love of God? Do our children and neighbors know from our lives and conversation that our treasure is in heaven—that we have an interest in Christ and His salvation? Or are they forced to conclude that our religion is a formality, and a sort of policy of insurance against possible fire in the future? Of how many professors of religion may it be said, "Thy speech betrayeth thee?"

THE TONGUE AN UNRULY MEMBER.

"Socrates relates a story of a plain, ignorant man who went to a learned man desiring to be taught a Psalm. He opened the Bible at the thirty-ninth Psalm and commenced reading to him, 'I said, I will take heed to my ways, that I sin not with my tongue.' He closed the book, saying he would learn that point first. After months of absence he was asked by his reader why he did not return. He answered that he had not yet learned his old lesson. And he gave the very same answer to one that asked him forty-nine years after."

CHAPTER LXIX.

SILENCE IS GOLDEN.

"I am working with a man who, desiring to provoke dispute, said, 'You have your belief and I have mine, but I do not believe the Bible.' "

The Christian made no reply, but "silently prayed" for his fellow workman. He said to a friend, "You should have seen the effect of silence upon him. We had no trouble and shall have none."

I have heard zealous Christians say, "I never allow a man to swear, use vulgar language or propagate infidel sentiments in my presence without rebuking him." Perhaps they have made a vow to that effect at a time of religious fervor.

Sin often needs rebuking at the time it is committed. But an invariable rule to do so may be too rigid. It does not give sufficient play for the exercise of sanctified judgment. A variety of persons and circumstances require great wisdom and humility in reproving sin.

"An inflexible rule" might reduce the Christian to an automaton. His service becoming stereotyped, might lack heart and spontaneity and fitness. The right thing may be done at the wrong time and place.

Silence in the presence of insults to Christ and ourselves may require more courage and self-control than speech. Silence might indicate zeal tempered with meekness and wisdom. It might manifest a degree of brotherliness and love not always found in prompt reply.

The Christian worker was not apathetic in the presence of sin, for he prayed for his companion; nor was he weak, for he sought to enlighten his ignorance.

The pastor said to the Christian man, "When you do speak he will listen with respect and weigh your words." Accustomed to being answered, and perhaps with spirit, he was trying your patience and the reality of your Christian faith and practice.

Perhaps he would make you angry and take the sweet unction to his soul that he is as good as you or any professor of religion. Then he might say, "They all get angry, talk back and live just as I do. If they are saved, so am I, and if they get to heaven, my chances are as good as theirs."

One Scripture says, "Answer not a fool according to his folly, lest thou be like unto him." But the next verse balances this: "Answer a fool according to his folly lest he be wise in his own conceit." Prov. 26: 4-5.

These Scriptures do not contradict, but complement each other. They mean, sometimes, answer foolish people, and at other times keep silence in the presence of their folly.

In deciding whether to speak or be silent we are to be led by providential openings, our sanctified common sense, the Word, the sense of "ought" and the Spirit of God. There is always a right way. And when we speak our words should be with grace seasoned with salt. We are to instruct those who oppose themselves in meekness of wisdom, considering ourselves lest we also be tempted.

LXX.

A CLOSING WORD.

We have come to the closing chapter. In reading the proof I have been afresh conscious of the limitations of the work.

But I have been inspired by a constant aim to be right. Some of the positions may be considered radical, but radical things are root things. Do you know that the Bible is an extreme book? Its teachings of holiness and sin; heaven and hell are so extreme that no human mind could conceive them.

We may look at life from the standpoint of the world. Amidst its jargon noises we may fail to hear the voice of God in the soul.

But when the angel which John the Revelator saw shall stand one foot upon the land and one upon the sea and declare "time was, time is but time shall be no longer," we shall view life differently. We shall appreciate its solemn meaning.

We shall not then feel that we have prayed too much, read the Bible too carefully, followed its precepts too strictly, given too much for God's cause, been too separate from sin, or too holy in heart and life.

Are we living the best we know? Are we walking in the light? Or, are we allowing sin in our lives? God sees. He knows. And we shall give account. We shall soon stand before the judgment seat of Christ.

Sinner, if you know that your sins are unpardoned flee to Jesus, the sinner's only refuge. Confess and forsake your sins and you will find mercy. The penitent soul need not fear. Jesus will abundantly pardon. He will save to the uttermost all who come to him.

Child of God are you oppressed with a sense of weakness and failure in the Christian life? As you found Jesus to be a pardoning Savior now trust Him to be your cleansing, keeping Savior. He will cleanse you from all sin. He will purify and make you whiter than snow. He will sanctify you wholly and give you victory amidst life's temptations and trials to the end. Only trust Him.

As I lay aside my pen I remember that I may never meet many of my readers on earth. One by one we shall drop from view and be seen no more of men. We are eternity bound.

MEET ME IN HEAVEN.

www.ingramcontent.com/pod-product-compliance
Lightning Source LLC
LaVergne TN
LVHW091030080826
845145LV00002B/432

* 9 7 8 1 6 2 1 7 1 6 0 1 3 *